Journey Through Ireland

by Terence Sheehy

HAMLYN

London · New York · Sydney · Toronto

Endpapers: The Crown Bar, Great Victoria
Street, Belfast
Title page: Moone High Cross
Title verso/Introduction: The falls at
Glenariff, County Antrim
Contents page: Atlantic Drive, County
Donegal

Editor: Donna Wood
Art Editor: Edward Pitcher
Designer: Marion Neville
Maps: Eugene Fleury
Production: Steve Roberts

Published 1986 by Hamlyn Publishing, a division of
The Hamlyn Publishing Group Limited, Bridge House,
London Road, Twickenham, Middlesex, England.

©Marshall Cavendish Limited 1986

ISBN 0 600 50251 1

The contents of this book are believed correct at the time
of printing. Nevertheless, the publisher can accept no
responsibility for errors or omissions or changes in the
details given.

Typeset in Palatino by TypeFast Ltd, London.
Printed in Italy by L.E.G.O. S.p.a. Vicenza.

Introduction

Everyone who has been there agrees that Ireland is unique. Its countryside, its castles, its shops and pubs have an atmosphere all of their own; it is a land of music, of legend and most of all, conversation. Everyone you meet seems to have kissed the Blarney Stone not once but several times. Whether you head straight for the elegant Georgian capital of Dublin or flee to the lush, green shores of the mighty River Shannon, head north to the spectacular Giant's Causeway in Antrim, or west to the rugged countryside of Connemara one thing is sure – you will love Ireland, and you'll want to return there again and again.

This book, with its vivid descriptions of Ireland's towns and villages, captures the magic of the country. Split into seven areas so that the special atmosphere of each region can be appreciated, famous landmarks, cities, and counties immortalised in song take their place alongside the lesser-known sites of this fascinating country.

Contents

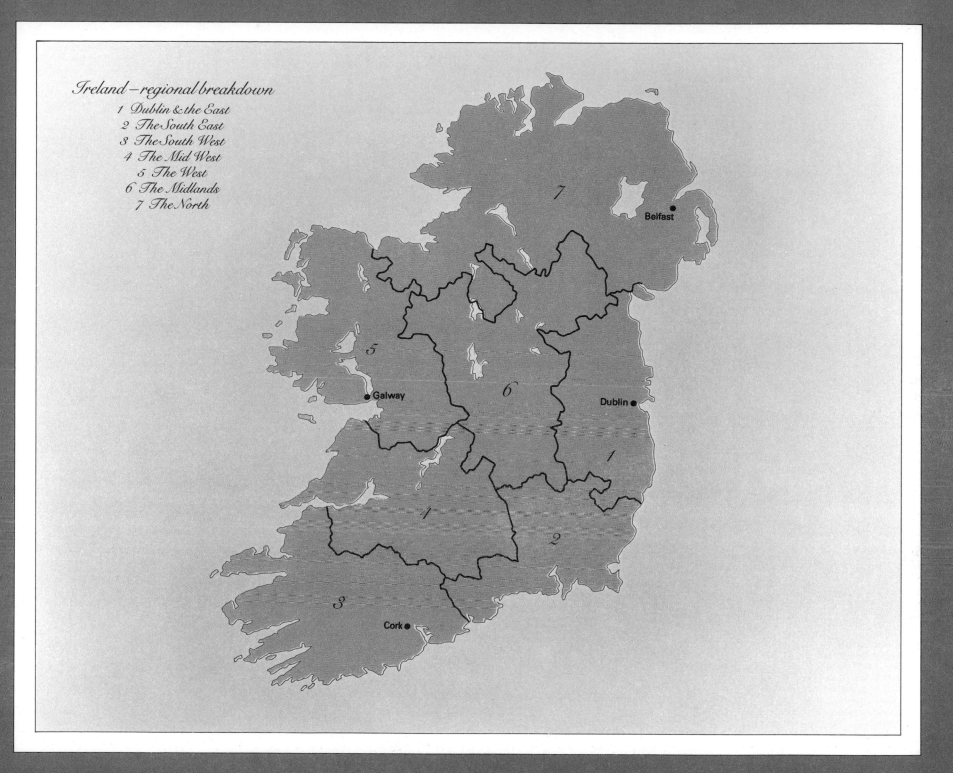

Ireland – regional breakdown
1 Dublin & the East
2 The South East
3 The South West
4 The Mid West
5 The West
6 The Midlands
7 The North

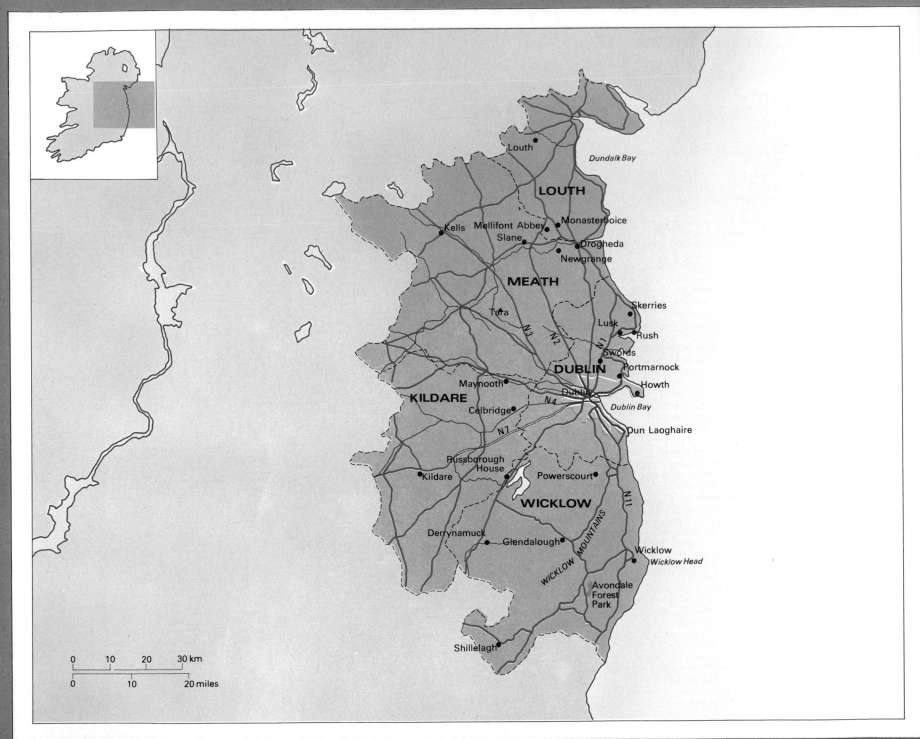

Louth

Dundalk Bay

LOUTH

Kells　Mellifont Abbey　Monasterboice
　　　Slane　Drogheda
　　　　Newgrange

MEATH

Tara　　Skerries
　　　Lusk
　　N3　N2　Rush
　　　　Swords
　　N1
DUBLIN　Portmarnock
Maynooth　　Howth
KILDARE　Dublin
Celbridge　N4
　　　　Dublin Bay
　　N7
　　　　Dun Laoghaire

Russborough
House
Kildare　　Powerscourt

WICKLOW　N11

Derrynamuck
　　Glendalough　WICKLOW MOUNTAINS
　　　　　Wicklow
　　　　　Wicklow Head
　　　Avondale
　　　Forest
　　　Park

Shillelagh

0　10　20　30 km

0　10　20 miles

Once the most elegant and fashionable of Georgian cities, Dublin retains many attractive features from that age. These Georgian doorways, with their distinctive fanlights and pillars, can be seen in many parts of the city

TOLEMY, THE GREEK geographer, referred to Dublin as 'Eblana', and put it on the map of the then-known world in A.D.140. Dublin derives its name from the Irish *Dubhlinn*, literally translated as the 'Dark Pool' (a reference to the Liffey).

Now, Dublin is the attractive and wealthy capital of Ireland, one of Europe's leading partners in trade in the European Common Market and a renowned cultural centre.

Dublin city stands on a bay, with arms of welcome outstretched from the Hill of Howth on the north side of the harbour of Dun Laoghaire, to 'the fort of Leary', formerly Kingstown, on the south side. To the east lies the lovely limestone plateau of Kildare, which produces some of the most valuable bloodstock in the world, and where there has been horseracing since before the time of Christ. To the south of Dublin are the picturesque blue granite-domed hills of Wicklow, with sandy strands and rocky headlands. To the north of Dublin are the rich fat cattle lands, the grasslands of 'Royal' Meath. 'Royal' Meath, because for centuries Tara of the Kings (an iron-age Celtic hill settlement) was the centre of government of Celtic Ireland, and because it is also the land of ancient royal underground graves and tumuli on the banks of the Boyne river and along its valley. Louth, 'the wee county', as it is affectionately known, is adjacent to Meath and is only 317 square miles in area.

AVONDALE FOREST PARK
County Wicklow

This Forestry Department-owned land of some 523 acres was once the estate and home of that celebrated and tragic leader of the Irish people, Charles Stewart Parnell. Here he was taught his Irish nationalism by his Irish-American mother. It lies along the superbly beautiful banks of the River Avondale.

Avondale House, built in 1777 is now the forestry school and its splendid architecture has been well preserved. Open to the public in the summer season, the guide, Mrs O'Connor, will show you the furniture and other articles belonging to Charles Stewart Parnell, and the beautiful hallway, the drawing room and the blue room with its ornamental plaster work of a very high standard.

There are nature trails through the enormous variety of trees.

AVONDALE FOREST PARK is approximately 35 miles south of Dublin city.

CELBRIDGE
County Kildare

Celbridge, a beautiful village on the River Liffey, was, at Celbridge Abbey, the home of Esther Vanhomrigh (1690-1723) immortalised in prose by Jonathan Swift as his ill-fated 'Vanessa'. At the eastern end of the village is what is arguably the most splendid Georgian country house in Ireland, Castletown House, open to the public, and built in 1722 for William Connolly, the speaker of the Irish House of Commons from 1715 to 1719. It is now the headquarters of the Irish Georgian Society. Two miles due north of Castletown House is Connolly's 'Folly',

St Lawrence's Gate, Drogheda — once there were nine others like it

140 ft in height, erected in 1740 by Connolly's widow to provide relief work for famine victims. It was designed by Richard Castle. Castletown House was the first of the great Palladian houses to be built in Ireland, and Connolly was the richest man of his time in Ireland. It set the pattern for other Palladian houses in Ireland with its central block linked by curved colonnades. The house was designed by the Italian architect Alessandro Galilei, and Bishop Berkeley was consulted about its design. Sir Edward Lovett Pearce, who designed the Irish Parliament House, had a large part in its building. The plasterwork in the house is by the Francini brothers, and the Long Gallery was decorated in the Pompeian manner by Thomas Riley in 1776. It has the only print room in Ireland, created by Lady Louisa Connolly and Lady Sarah Napier in 1775. It has a wealth of Irish Furniture and art treasures.

CELBRIDGE is 13 miles due west of Dublin, a journey which Jonathan Swift so often made on horseback to visit his beloved 'Vanessa'.

DERRYNAMUCK
County Wicklow

The remote, wild beauty of Wicklow County is best seen on the Glen of Imaal road, five miles of hills that rise to more than 1000 ft leading to the thatched cottage at Derrynamuck where Michael Dwyer, rebel leader of 1798, was trapped by Redcoats and saved by his comrade Sam MacAllister, who was killed as he drew the soldiers' fire. The cottage is furnished and restored to its 18th-century appearance.

DERRYNAMUCK is best approached by the Dublin to Hollywood road, via Donard. It is about 38 miles south west of Dublin.

DROGHEDA
County Louth

Drogheda, the 'Bridge of the Ford', is an important and ancient town which spans the River Boyne. It was built by the Norse Sea King Turgesius in 911, and the Normans made it a fortress town. Here Richard II secured the submission of O'Neill, Prince of Ulster and other

The Four Courts at Dublin, designed by James Gandon

Irish chieftains in 1395. In 1649, when Cromwell stormed the town, he personally ordered the butchery of some 2000 of its defenders and sent the rest into slavery in the Barbadoes. The St Lawrence Gate is the only remaining 13th-century one of the original ten.

St Peter's Church, in West Street, was erected in memory of St Oliver Plunkett, (1629-1681), Archbishop of Armagh, who was hanged, drawn and quartered at Tyburn in London in 1681. His embalmed head, blackened by fire, is preserved in a special shrine on an altar in the north transept.

🚗 *DROGHEDA is 30 miles north of Dublin.*

DUBLIN
County Dublin

Dublin has all the pros and cons of a capital city. To the average Dubliner it is one of the most attractive places to live, with two major racecourses in its suburbs, 30 golf courses within half an hour's drive of the city centre and safe bays and beaches only minutes away. It has an east-west axis of the River Liffey and is very definitely divided into a north side and a south side. O'Connell Street is the main street of the city, straddling the river at O'Connell Bridge.

In European or World terms Dublin is a village, and a relatively small village, with one main street. That is its real attraction, it can be walked, and its treasures of architecture and art visited on foot in a matter of hours. Like all modern cities it has an impossible traffic situation. It is very much a city of the young and a centre of learning, as it boasts two major universities; the modern National University of Ireland, University College Dublin, and the Elizabethan foundation of the College of the Holy and Undivided Trinity.

On the high ground on which the city rose is the magnificent cathedral of Christchurch, founded by the Danes and rebuilt by the Normans under Strongbow in 1172. His tomb and that of his son can be seen today. Dubliners rejoice in the fact that this Norman cathedral was restored by a wealthy whiskey distiller, Henry Roe, while St Patrick's Gothic Cathedral, built in 1190, was restored by a wealthy brewer, Sir Benjamin Lee Guinness.

Down on the quays, near Dublin's Four Courts, in Church Street, is the Church of St Michan, founded in 1096. Handel played the organ there, and in its vaults are the mummified bodies of centuries-old citizens of Dublin, so old that you can, if you so desire, shake hands with a dead Crusader.

The real flavour of Georgian Dublin can be savoured in College Green, where stands the Old Parliament House, now the headquarters of the Bank of Ireland. The work of Lovett Pearce, Surveyor-General of Ireland in 1729, and of James Gandon, who made additions in 1785, its Parliamentary days heard the greatest of Irish orators such as Henry Grattan, and it closed in 1800 when the Act of Union united the British and Irish parliaments in London. Across the road stands Trinity College whose magnificent buildings include the Examination Hall, the Library, the Chapel, and the Printing House, all erected between 1722 and 1732. On the corner of Grafton Street stands one of the most attractive residences in Europe, the Provost's House, built in 1760.

Trinity College Library dates from 1601. By an Act of Parliament in 1801 it has a right to a copy of every book printed in Ireland and in Britain, so its books and manuscripts run into millions. Its greatest treasure, on view to the public, is the 8th-century illuminated manuscript of the gospels, the *Book of Kells*. The most valuable book in the world, it is insured for £10 million. Dublin is a city for book lovers, for the National Library of Ireland in Kildare Street contains over half a million books and hundreds of thousands of prints and Irish newspapers and maps. The Royal Irish Academy Library in Dawson Street houses an extensive collection of rare manuscripts from the 6th to the 16th centuries, and Marsh's Library, adjacent to St Patrick's Cathedral, and open to the public, was founded in 1707 by Archbishop Marsh. The oldest library in the country, it contains tens of thousands of rare volumes and manuscripts. Also open to the public is the Sir Chester Beatty Library, at 20 Shrewsbury Road, with the most valuable collection of Oriental manuscripts in the world.

Trinity College, Dublin, seen from the Bank of Ireland

Despite its Victorian 'glass-case' presentation of antiquities, the National Museum in Kildare Street contains one of the finest collections of Celtic gold objects in Europe. The most famous exhibits are the Tara Brooch, the Ardagh Chalice, the Cross of Cong and St Patrick's Bell and Bell Shrine. In recent times an 8th-century addition has been made in the shape of the Derrynaflan Chalice. There is always some precious antiquity being unearthed in the bog-lands of Ireland. For lovers of the visual arts there are two important Art Galleries. The first is the National Gallery in Merrion Square opened in 1864 and containing over 2000 treasures. The

Irish Room with the works of John Butler Yeats, Hone, Osborne, Lavery, Orpen, Tuohy, Roderick O'Conor, Jack Yeats and Paul Henry gives a cross-section of the works of Ireland's greatest painters. The National Gallery is financed by funds from the estate of George Bernard Shaw in memory of the many happy days of his youth spent there.

Equally important in the world of art is the Municipal Gallery of Modern Art in Parnell Square, founded by Sir Hugh Lane, famous for his collection of French Impressionist paintings. He drowned in the sinking of the *Lusitania*, and his will, leaving his collection of pictures to the Municipal Gallery in

Dublin, was disputed because legally its codicil lacked two witnesses. Due to the efforts of Lord Longford an amicable settlement was reached so that half of his collection is on view in Dublin and the other half in London, changing every five years. The Municipal Gallery is important because its works give a visual glimpse of modern Ireland's history.

Dublin is renowned for its Georgian character, but while many of its wide streets and squares and lovely Georgian doorways remain, a devil-may care attitude in modern times towards things Georgian has left much of it to decay. The steel and glass facades of modern office blocks and hotels now spoil the looks of a once elegant town.

It is understandable that the Irish people of today should have no love for a Georgian age which is associated with deportation and famine, and an alien and absent landlord class. However, much remains from that time that is good. Leinster House is a glorious Georgian mansion in Kildare Street, now the assembly place of the politicians of Ireland, the elected deputies of the Dáil, the Chamber of Deputies, and of the Seanad House, Senate or Upper House. Leinster House, built in 1745, was the town house of the Duke of Leinster. As first Duke, he built it in its solitary state on indifferent marshy land far from the popular north side of Dublin, and boasted that the fashionable would follow him across the Liffey. They did. The style of his building was copied too. The White House in Washington D.C. is modelled on Leinster House.

The Abbey theatre in Abbey Street is one of the most magnificent centres of drama in the world. The old building, built on the unpromising site of the city morgue, was opened in 1904 and burnt to the ground in 1951. The new 1966 building is functional but the glory is in the lobby where hang the portraits in oils of the 'greats' such as Yeats, Synge, O'Casey, Lennox Robinson, George Shiels, Denis Johnston and Lady Gregory.

The world-renowned Royal Dublin Society was founded in 1731 at Ballsbridge. Every year in the first week in August the Dublin Horseshow is staged in its grounds.

In Phoenix Park Dublin can boast the most beautiful enclosed public park in the world, all 1760 acres of it, with its Polo grounds open to the public, its charming Zoological Gardens and its 200 acres of playing fields, once famous as duelling grounds.

The Shelbourne Hotel has been for well over a century a window on the everyday passing parade of the capital city. It resounds to the talk and the chatter of fashionable people, of politicians on the make, of 'Horse Protestants' up from the country, from their great houses, of hunting men and women, and, in August, the International Show jumping teams of the world.

It is very Irish. It looks down on Iveagh House, the headquarters of the Irish Department of Foreign Affairs. Its rooms have views right

Marsh's Library is full of rare, old volumes

The elegant facade of the Shelbourne Hotel, frequented by Dublin's literati 7

across the city to the Dublin hills, and to the blue Wicklow mountains. The Dail — the Irish Parliament, meets around the corner. And here too are Government buildings, the National Art Gallery, the National Museum and the National Library. It is a stone's throw from the fashionable walk-about shopping centre that is in Grafton Street, and the Lord Mayor's Mansion House.

As Conrad Hilton said, a successful hotel requires three things; position, position and position. The Shelbourne has all three requirements. Thackeray stayed there in 1842, when it was owned by that splendid Tipperary patriot, Martin Burke. Said William Makepeace of the hotel it is 'much frequented by families from the country . . . majestically conducted by clerks and other officers.' It hasn't changed much. The staff are delightful and helpful Dubliners and the service is superb, although, in Thackeray's day the window of his room was propped open with a broom!

During the 1916 Rising they continued to serve splendid afternoon teas at the Shelbourne, despite the bullets flying from the College of Surgeons, where Countess Markievicz, the former debutante Constance Gore-Booth was in command in a green uniform.

It had great days when it was managed by Captain Peter Jury, always referred to as 'The Captain', who inherited it from his father 'The Colonel', who commanded his regiment, the 18th Royal Hussars, Queen Mary's Own.

Now, after a £4 million face-lift it is one of the best hotels in Ireland with a special Irish flavour and welcome of its very own.

St Patrick's Cathedral contains the death mask, a magnificent bust and the epitaph of Dean Swift, and the

The magnificent interior of St Patrick's Cathedral

altar and the pulpit he used. Made dean in 1713, author Jonathan Swift died in 1745 after terrible mental illness, and lies buried in the south west nave, near his beloved Stella. A brass plate marks the grave.

On the south wall is his bust, and to its right, above the doorway, is the epitaph he wrote. In translation it reads:

"Here lies the body of Jonathan Swift, Doctor of Divinity, Dean of this Cathedral Church, where fierce indigna-

tion can no longer rend the heart. Go, traveller, and imitate if you can, this earnest and dedicated champion of liberty. 1745 A.D. Aged 78 years".

To capture the glamour and atmosphere of the eternal calvalcade that is Dublin, a quiet stroll, or a seat in St Stephen's Green, in its centre, off the fashionable promenade of Grafton Street, will provide a glimpse of the passing parade of a young city which James Joyce immortalised and through whose

streets strolled men such as Jonathan Swift, George Farquhar, George Berkeley, Edmund Burke, Oliver Goldsmith, Richard Brinsley Sheridan, Thomas Moore, James Clarence Mangan, George Moore, Oscar Wilde, George Bernard Shaw, William Butler Yeats, John Millington Synge, Sean O'Casey and Brendan Behan. Dublin has long been a place of inspiration for writers.

DUBLIN is 160 miles north east of Cork, 104 miles south of Belfast.

James Joyce's Dublin

James Joyce, born in Dublin on 2 February 1882, immortalised the city in *Ulysses*. Said Joyce of this book: 'I want to give a picture of Dublin so complete that if the city one day suddenly disappeared from the earth it could be reconstructed out of my book.' In his *Finnegan's Wake*, the River Liffey was captured forever in splendid prose as 'Anna Livia Plurabelle. In his *Dubliners*, and his *Portrait of the Artist as a Young Man*, he caught the atmosphere of the pubs of Dublin, the gaiety of Grafton Street, the squalor of the dingy lanes, the 'surly front' of Trinity College, the dignity of the National Library, and recalled the happy times spent at the Martello Tower at Sandycove, now the James Joyce Museum, which he shared with St John Gogarty, the 'Buck Mulligan' of *Ulysses*.

His residences in the Dublin area included 41 Brighton Square, Rathgar, his birthplace; 23 Castlewood Avenue, Rathmines; 1 Martello Terrace, Bray, County Wicklow; 23 Carysfort Avenue, Blackrock, County Dublin; 2 Millbourne Avenue, Drumcondra; 29 Windsor Avenue, Fairview; 8 Royal Terrace, Fairview, 32 Glengariff Parade, off the North Circular Road; and 7 St Peter's Terrace, Cabra.

He attended the Jesuit school of Clongowes Wood and Belvedere College, Dublin, and graduated from the old Royal University in 1898. He died in Zurich in 1941.

James Joyce was a regular in Dublin's pubs

Many streets have hardly changed since Joyce's time

DUN LAOGHAIRE
County Dublin

Formerly named 'Kingstown' in 1821, to commemorate the visit of King George IV to Ireland, the town has reverted to its old Irish name which means the Fort of Laoghaire (pronounced 'Leary'). The great harbour, today the principal sea-link with Britain, was begun in 1817 by John Rennie. It took more than 50 years to build, and covers over 250 acres between its massive granite piers quarried from the nearby Dalkey hills. A major yachting centre, it is the home of several yacht clubs. It is also the base of the Irish Lights Service. The East pier is a delightful promenade. Just one and a quarter miles further south is the James Joyce Martello Tower, which features in *Ulysses*, now a Joycean museum.

Killiney Bay, four miles south of Dun Laoghaire, is popularly known as the Irish Bay of Naples. George Bernard Shaw lived in adjacent Dalkey in Torca cottage, from 1866 to 1874. The Vico road connects Killiney Hill and Dalkey hill and the view from the 500 ft high summit of Killiney affords a magnificent panoramic vista of the sea and the surrounding countryside. At Monkstown, a suburb on the Dublin side of Dun Laoghaire, in Belgrave Square, the Irish Culture Institute, (*Comalthas Ceoltoiri Eireann*) present the most splendid traditional Irish music and dance in summer.

🚗 *DUN LAOGHAIRE is 8 miles south of Dublin.*

GLENDALOUGH
County Wicklow

Glendalough was founded by St Kevin in the 6th century. He came there first to live as a hermit but his sanctity and fame attracted so many people to him that he set up a monastery, and died there at the age of 125 years of age. The monastery became a European university in A.D. 617. Burnt nine times, and pillaged by the Norse raiders three times in the 9th and 10th centuries, it was plundered by the Normans, inundated by a great flood in 1174 and was re-established as a diocese in 1450. It remained beyond the King's Writ in the mountain fortress of Wicklow when the O'Byrne and O'Toole clans held the county against the central government in Dublin. Once a famous centre of pilgrimage it fell silent and deserted, and the wonder is that such a diversity of stone buildings survive.

After St Kevin, Glendalough had one period of glory when St Laurence O'Toole was appointed Abbot in 1153, and became Archbishop of Dublin in 1161. He was a powerful figure and tried to negotiate with the English King Henry II, in France, about his deportation of Roderic O'Connor, high King of Ireland. St Laurence died at Eu, in Normandy and was canonized in 1226.

The monastic settlement and university covers one and a half miles of the valley. Its farthest point is on the Upper Lake, Temple-na-Skellig 'The Church of the Rock', a small, rectangular church standing on a shelf 20ft above the water. It features a twin light east window. On the platform the original wood and mud hut of St Kevin would have stood. St Kevin's Bed, east of Temple-na-Skellig, is a cave 30 ft above the lake level, 4 ft wide, 7 ft deep and 3½ ft high. It was probably a Bronze Age burial place before St Kevin used it.

Reefert Church, — 'The King's Burial Place' — is the burial place of the O'Toole clan, on the south east corner of the Upper Lake, near the Poulanass Waterfall. The ruins of the church date from the 11th century. Near Reefert are the foundations of another church about 35 ft long and with walls 3 ft thick. Along the Upper and Lower Lake are various ancient stone crosses. In the fields west of the graveyard of the monastic university city is Our Lady's Church, the earliest church in the valley with a remarkable west doorway of seven massive blocks of granite. On slightly higher ground, north-west of the cathedral, is the almost perfect Round Tower. Composed of local granite and mica-slate it has six storeys. The doorway is 12 ft above the ground and the whole unique Irish defence tower against hit-and-run Norse raiders has been standing for over 1000 years. The arched gateway to the monastic settlement is the only one of its kind in Ireland. The Priest's House, within the cemetery, was a burial place for local clergy in penal times. Standing between the Priest's House and the Cathedral is the 11 ft high St Kevin's Cross. The largest ruins are of the 11th-century Cathedral. They consist of a nave, chancel and sacristy. St Kevin's Church, popularly known as 'St Kevin's Kitchen', is a perfect example of a barrel-vaulted church with high pitched stone roofs and a miniature Round Tower bell tower. The Church of St Kieran, 12 yards south east of St Kevin's church is a foundation of a nave and a chancel, and commemorates the founder of the monastic university of Clonmacnoise. St Saviour's priory, east of the Round Tower, was founded by St Laurence O'Toole in 1162.

In 1985 eight Benedictine monks from Canada arrived in Glendalough to begin anew its monastic tradition.

Glendalough's almost perfect Round Tower is over 1000 years old and made from local granite

🚗 *GLENDALOUGH is 32 miles from Dublin.*

HOWTH
County Dublin

On the north side of Dublin Bay, Howth derives its name from the Norse name *Höfud*, meaning a head. Its Irish name is *Beann Eadair*, Edar's Peak, 565 ft in height. From its summit is a breathtaking panoramic view, north to the Mountains of Mourne, and south to the Wicklow Mountains. It was originally meant to be the Holyhead-Dublin sea link, built between 1801 and 1810. However, the harbour silted up, the architect committed suicide, and the mail boat station was transferred to Dun Laoghaire. St Mary's Church is on the site of the first church built in 1042 by Sitric, the Norse King of Dublin. The present church is basically 14th century and contains the tomb of the St Lawrence family, the Lords of Howth. Howth Castle and Demesne has been the seat of the St Lawrence family since 1600. The Lords of Howth follow a custom of always setting a place for a stranger at table, even to this day, to avoid a curse placed on the family by Grace O'Malley, the Irish sea queen pirate of Elizabethan days. She was returning from the court of Elizabeth and found the castle gates closed against her at evening meal time. In revenge she kidnapped the St Lawrence heir and only returned him on condition that their gates would never again be locked against the stranger seeking hospitality. The gardens are rich in rhododendra and azaleas and open to the public. Below the Hill of

Howth is the Bailey Lighthouse, erected in 1814, on the site of the Cromlech of King Crimthan who died in the first century A.D. The village is famous for its seafood restaurants and for the best traditional ballad sessions in Ireland at the Abbey Tavern Restaurant. Ireland's Eye, like a sleeping cat, lies two miles north east of Howth, once the settlement of St Nessan. It was plundered time and time again by raiding Norsemen.

🚗 *HOWTH is 9½ miles north of Dublin city.*

KELLS
County Meath

Kells, its ancient name *Ceanannus Mór*, The Great Residence, is a historic market town in the delightfully wooded valley of the River Blackwater. It was the site of one of the most important 16th-century monastic university settlements founded by the great St Colmcille in the 6th century. St Colmcille moved to Iona, and founded a monastic settlement there. In the 8th century his monks returned, driven out by the Viking raiders from Iona. The monastery was pillaged and burnt by the Vikings in 919, in 950 and again in 969. The greatest 9th-century treasure of the monastery was its *Book of Kells*, an illuminated manuscript of the Four Gospels, in Latin, stolen or hidden in the earth in 1007, which is now in the library of Trinity College, Dublin, and valued at £10 million. In the wars between the native Irish and the Normans the monastery was burnt down in 1111 and again in 1156. The Synod of Kells, held there in 1152, set up the provinces of Armagh, Cashel, Dublin and Tuam. It then became a Norman fortress. On top of the hill is the Round Tower

The intricately carved High Cross at Kells

and a collection of Celtic High Crosses. The Round Tower, minus its conical cap, is 100 ft high and has five windows at its top pointing to the five ancient roads that lead to the town. Murchadh Mac Flainn, High King of Ireland, was slain in this tower in 1076. Next to the Round Tower is the Celtic High Cross called the South Cross, erected in the 9th century, and dedicated to St Columba and St Patrick. The Celtic interlacing on the base depicts various animals, including a deer and a chariot procession. The south face depicts Adam and Eve, Cain and Abel, and other biblical scenes, and the arms too are richly carved, as are the ends of the cross. The west side depicts Christ in Judgement and the Crucifixion. There are three other crosses in the graveyard, and the fifth, 9 ft high, richly sculpted, is the Market Cross

standing in the middle of the town. St Colmcille's House was built about 805 to commemorate the return of St Colmcille's monks from Iona. This monastic building is very similar in design to St Kevin's church in Glendalough in County Wicklow. Just six miles from Kells is the Hill of Tailte, at Teltown. On this hill once stood *Rath Dubh*, the Black Fort, which was once the ancient palace of the High King Tuathal.

🚗 *KELLS is 40 miles north west of Dublin, 10 miles from Navan, and 15 miles from Slane.*

KILDARE
County Kildare

Kildare, from the Irish *Cill Dara*, the church of the oak, is forever associated with St Brigid. Tradition says a vast oak tree once stood where the present Cathedral of Kildare now stands. In 490 Brigid, the greatest female saint Ireland has ever produced, built her monastery here and its church became the centre of Christendom in the Kingdom of Leinster. As Abbess St Brigid established the monastery for her nuns, while St Conlaed, as Abbot Bishop, ruled over a separate section for his monks. The whole edifice was divided down the middle, and, continuing an old pagan practice on the site, a perpetual flame was kept burning. The Norsemen plundered the shrines of Brigid and Conlaed in 835, and it was burnt down again in 1050 and in 1067. The Normans built a Franciscan Abbey in 1260, funded by the de Vesci family. By the 1480s the Cathedral had been fully repaired and decorated to be reduced to ruins again in the Confederate wars. In Victorian times the Cathedral was over-restored to its present state. Close to the Cathedral is a magnificently preserved Round Tower, which

The tension mounts as spectators fill the Curragh Racecourse in Kildare

rises to a height of 105 ft.

Kildare is a busy market town with an Irish Army garrison with ornate iron entrance gates, and is a prosperous centre for the Irish horse breeding and training industry with 35 racing stables. The vast limestone grassy plain east of the town of Kildare, 5000 acres of world famous turf, six miles long and two miles wide, has seen classic horseracing there since the time when the gods of Greece were young. In the centre of this domed limestone plain is the Curragh Camp, the West Point or Sandhurst of Ireland, which contains a splendid garrison Church of St Brigid, with works of modern Irish art. All around the Curragh are world famous racing stables and one of the most glorious and poetic sights in Ireland is in the mists of the early morning when the various stable's thoroughbreds are at exercise, at the trot, at the gallop and flat out over the hallowed turf. The Curragh Racecourse is the scene of the Irish Derby, run by the Irish Hospital Sweepstakes with the largest prize money in the world of horseracing, and other Irish Classics such as the Irish 1000 guineas, 2000 guineas, the Irish Oaks and the Irish St Leger. At Tully, a mile south of Kildare town, and open to the public, is the Irish Government's National Stud, where horses worth millions of dollars or pounds are based. There is an excellent museum attached to the National Stud illustrating the history of horseracing in Ireland from earliest times. Adjacent to the National Stud are the Japanese Gardens which symbolise the life of man from birth to death. At the eastern end of the Curragh is Donnelly's Hollow, where a small obelisk commemorates the barefoot boxing victory of the giant Irishman, Dan Donnelly over the English box-

World-class horses are bred at Kildare's National Stud

ing champion George Cooper.

🚗 *KILDARE is 33 miles south west of Dublin.*

LOUTH
County Louth

Now only a tiny village of the 'wee county', as County Louth is affectionately known, (it is Ireland's smallest county, covering only 317 square miles) Louth is nevertheless of great importance, for St Patrick built the original church here and appointed his disciple, St Mochta, who died in 535, as its first bishop. St Mochta's House, beside the village, probably 10th century, is 18 ft long and 10 ft wide with a high-pitched stone roof. It has an upper and lower storey. St Mary's Abbey, once a Dominican friary, and also beside the village, dates from 1148 when the Prince of Oriel Donough O'Carroll endowed it. The 14th-century ruins are all that remain of what was once a church 150 ft long and 50 ft wide.

One mile east of the village at Ardpatrick, St Patrick founded a church, and in Ardpatrick House lived St Oliver Plunkett, to whom it was given by his kinsman, Lord Louth. Two miles north east of Louth, east of the Dundalk road at Rathneety, is the 12 ft high Clocha-fearmor Standing Stone, which legend associates with the death of Cucchailainn, the mythical hero of old Irish. Cucchailainn 'The Hound of Ulster', mortally wounded, tied himself to this standing stone to face his countless enemies of the army of Queen Maeve of Connacht. Close to death, he stuck to his belief that it is better to have one day of glorious valour than to have a life of mediocrity. His enemies kept their distance and not until the raven of death perched on his shoulder did they dare to approach him. This scene is dramatically captured in the bronze statue of Cucchailainn, by Oliver Sheppard, that stands today in the General Post Office in O'Connell Street in Dublin, as a memorial to the volunteers who fought in the Rising in 1916.

🚗 *LOUTH village is 8 miles south west of Dundalk, which is 52 miles north of Dublin on the main road to Belfast.*

LUSK
County Dublin

This village boasts a well-preserved 8th-century Round Tower, 100ft in height, a classic example of the Irish defence against hit-and-run Norse raiders. Lusk was founded in the 5th century by St Mac Cuilinn who lived a hermit's life in the local cave, the Irish word for cave being *Lusca*. To the Round Tower the Normans added a square tower with round towers at three corners, to which was added a medieval church. The monastic settlement of the 9th century was burnt and pillaged by raiding Norsemen on at least two occasions. The church contains the medieval tomb of the Barnewalls of Turvey, (1589) and of the Berminghams of Ballough, 1527 and 1589. There is a magnificent view of north County Dublin; *Fingal*, the land of the Fair Strangers, from the top of the five-story Round Tower.

The present Catholic church has fine stained-glass windows by the Irish artist Harry Clarke.

🚗 *LUSK is 11 miles north of Dublin City.*

MAYNOOTH
County Kildare

Maynooth stands alongside the old Royal Canal, on the main Dublin to Galway road. At the west end of the

The product of many additions throughout the ages, the church at Lusk

village are the massive ruins and gate of the Geraldine Castle, built by Maurice FitzGerald in 1176, one of Strongbow's original adventurer invaders. The Geraldine Earls of Kildare lived here in considerable style until 1535 when the rebel Silken Thomas was taken after a siege by Sir William Skeffington, Henry VIII's deputy in Ireland, who used siege guns for the very first time in Irish history. Betrayed by his foster mother, Silken Thomas and his entire garrison were given the Tudor 'Pardon of Maynooth', which meant that they were beheaded!

The Gate Tower is now the entrance to the Pontifical University which is St Patrick's College, Maynooth, one of the largest Catholic colleges in the world dedicated to the university education of priests who go out to the missions all over the globe, as well as serving the people of Ireland. The present college dates from 1795 and incorporates the original Stoyte House of the steward to the Duke of Leinster, a magnificent Georgian house. The vast university buildings, sprawling in all directions, include the magnificent college chapel which is the work of Pugin and his pupil J.J. Mc-Carthy. Among its many treasures is an enormous solid silver statue of St George and the Dragon and a cloth-of-gold set of vestments decorated with shamrocks. These were presented to the then all-male establishment in 1878 by Elizabeth, Empress of Austria, who was on a hunting holiday in the neighbourhood and came in, on a horse, over the wall. The nationalist priests, although impressed by her entrance, were not too flattered to be given a statue of the patron saint of England.

Of the many illustrious alumni of the college probably the best known 15 were the rebel Archbishop of Melbourne, Daniel Mannix, president of the college from 1903 to 1912, and the one-time lecturer in mathematics, Eammon De Valera, later to become President of Ireland. Now open to lay students, both men and women, the new campus on the west side of the college is an interesting layout of modern architecture. Visitors are admitted in the holiday times of the students and one of the unusual attractions is the 'Ghost Room', where two students committed suicide in the mid-19th century. The room had to be exorcised, and the corridor wall removed, to make it wide-open to the public. An altar has been placed in the room. Among Maynooth's many artistic treasures is an enormous carved limestone head of St Patrick carved by the Cork sculptor, Seamus Murphy, author of *Stone Mad*.

MAYNOOTH is 15 miles west of Dublin, on the main road to Mullingar and Athlone.

MELLIFONT ABBEY
County Louth

St Malachi of Armagh, student friend of the great St Bernard of Ciairvaux, founded the first Cistercian monastery in Ireland here in 1142. Donogh O'Carroll, King of Uriel granted the land, and St Bernard sent his architect and mastermason, Robert, to assist in building the church. The Gate House, a massive square tower, still stands over 50 ft in height, and four arches of the spectacular 12th-century lavabo also still stand. This was the first of some 35 Cistercian monasteries in Ireland which brought with them a strong continental influence on Irish life.

MELLIFONT is 4 miles west of Drogheda.

16

Monasterboice's Round Tower was once the tallest in Ireland

MONASTERBOICE
County Louth

Monasterboice's Round Tower, although its top storey is missing, still stands 100 ft high, and was the tallest in Ireland in its heyday. There are the remains of a 9th-century church, the South church, and adjacent to the Round Tower the remains of the North church. The most splendid example of a sculptured 9th-century Celtic cross is Muireadach's Cross, nearly 18 ft high, and still standing at the entrance to the graveyard. It is of superb design and workmanship with a central figure of Christ crucified on the west side and the Last Judgement on the east side. The rest of both faces is a multiplicity of scenes from the scriptures interlaced with animals and hunters. The West Cross is 21½ ft high, highly ornate, and the North Cross, similarly carved, is 16 ft high. There is also a monastic sundial carved in granite.

MONASTERBOICE is 6 miles north west of Drogheda, 1 mile west of the main road to Dundalk.

NEWGRANGE
County Meath

At Newgrange is Ireland's most spectacular and finest prehistoric monument and arguably the best passage grave in Europe. It is a burial mound 42 ft high, 300 ft in diameter, and dating from 2500 B.C. It was once ringed by 38 boulders with an average height of 8 ft, of which a dozen remain. At the base of the underground grave are huge, horizontally lying stones with intricate geometric designs carved on them in triple spiral form, in double circles and semi-circles and diamond shaped carvings. There is more than a hint of an Indian origin in these designs. It is probable that the burial mound served as a primitive observatory as there are carvings of the course of the moon and the stars. The passage into the centre of the burial chamber is 62 ft long, and the central chamber is cruciform in shape. The dead would have been cremated and their ashes placed in the stone basin on the floor. Spirals, zig-zags and lozenges decorate the stones in the passageway which has two burial chambers in addition to the corbelled-roofed, 10 ft-high main burial chamber. Very recently the carved head of what was probably a druidic chieftain's stick or wand was discovered, and archaeologists still have lots to learn about this burial place of Kings. The whole of this historic area of the Boyne Valley is known as *Brugh na Boinne*, 'The Palace of the Boyne', and a mile or two away are the equally fascinating burial mounds of Knowth and of Dowth. Knowth is 40 ft high and 220 ft in diameter, and is a satellite of Newgrange. Dowth is 50 ft high and 280 ft in diameter and also contains ritual stone basins and prehistoric tombs on both sides of the main tomb. The kerb stones all share the mystic spiral carvings of Indian origin.

🚗 *NEWGRANGE is roughly 30 miles north west of Dublin and a few miles east of Slane.*

PORTMARNOCK
County Dublin

Portmarnock has three miles of sandy strand from which the Irish Army Colonel Fitzmaurice and his German companions took off in a Junker's plane to make the first east-west Atlantic crossing.

St Doulagh's Church, two miles west of Portmarnock, is little known, and yet it was the 6th-

Strange carvings decorate stones within fascinating Newgrange passage grave

Quiet and unspoilt, Rush has two sandy beaches and a fishing harbour

century hermit cell of St Doulagh. The old rectangular vaulted church is 13th century and the square tower is presumed to rise above the burial place of the saint. St Doulagh's Well is enclosed by an octagonal stone roof. Adjacent is St Catherine's Well, an underground chamber with a strange sunken bath about 3ft deep. Nearby is St Doulagh's Lodge, once the home of Nathaniel Hone, Ireland's most famous landscape painter of his era, who lived from 1831 to 1917. A Barbizon painter, who had studied with Millet, he was a distinguished member of the Royal Hibernian Academy.

The town has an 18 hole world championship golf course.

PORTMARNOCK *is 9 miles north of Dublin.*

POWERSCOURT
County Wicklow

Quite the most beautiful gardens in Ireland are those of the 14,000 acre Powerscourt Demesne on either side of the banks of the lovely Dargle River. The great house, once the home of Viscount Powerscourt, was badly damaged by fire, but the chief glory are the gardens. As in classical Chinese gardens they blend, deliberately, with the magnificent backdrop of the Sugar Loaf mountain, which looks like a minor Vesuvius. The gardens, complete with formal lake, fountains, trees and shrubs were 30 years in the making and were finished in 1875. The spectacular circular terraces descend to the Triton Lake, which is guarded by winged horses rampant. Daniel Robertson, who originally laid out the formal gardens, had over 100 gardeners to assist him. Arthur Young, the celebrated 18th-century agriculturalist who frequently stayed at Powerscourt said, quite simply, that it was the most beautiful place in the world. The Japanese gardens were added by the 8th Viscount in 1908 from reclaimed bogland. Many of the trees of the Demesne were planted over 200 years ago and came from all over the world. Some stand over 150 ft high. Roses and rhododendrons, magnolia and azalea grow in great profusion. The famous

Oriental splendour in the gardens of Powerscourt estate. These gardens took 30 years to perfect

Powerscourt Waterfall is one of the highest in Ireland, dropping a spectacular 400 ft. There are herds of deer in the park. Added attractions are an armoury museum, and a gift shop and restaurant, superbly managed by one of Ireland's former leading lady equestrian show jumpers.

POWERSCOURT is 4 miles south west of Bray.

RUSH
County Dublin

Rush has a charming fishing harbour, two beautiful sandy strands and a 9-hole golf links which looks over the island of Lambay and south over Dublin Bay. Its name in Irish, *Ros Eo*, means the peninsular of the yew, and local tradition holds that many of the bows used at Agincourt came from this headland. It is the market garden for Dublin, because its light, sandy soil yields many annual crops. Its people are largely descended from the Norsemen of north Dublin and work with Scandinavian ardour.

The Catholic church of Saint Maur, now being re-built, was originally built by Breton sailors as a thanksgiving for their being saved from a shipwreck off Lambay Island where fierce currents rage.

RUSH is 18 miles north of Dublin.

RUSSBOROUGH HOUSE
County Wicklow

Russborough, at Blessington, is the perfect Palladian style house of two of the most generous supporters of

the arts in Ireland, Sir Alfred and Lady Beit. A gleaming Wicklow granite mansion, it was built in 1741 for Joseph Leeson by the architect Richard Cassels. Today it stands with almost every detail of its original baroque plasterwork, wood-work, floors and mantels intact. The house is the perfect setting for Sir Alfred Beit's collection of priceless paintings, furniture and objets d'art. The art collection includes Magnacos, Murillos, Velazquez, Gainsboroughs, Raeburns, Guardis, Vermeers, and a superb Goya, his portrait of the dancer Dona Antonia Zarate. The facade of the imposing house embraces a central building joined by curving colonnades to buildings to the east and to the west. The house has the added advantage of overlooking the Poulaphouca reservoir.

RUSSBOROUGH HOUSE is 3 miles south east of the beautiful village of Blessington, which is 18 miles south of Dublin.

SHILLELAGH
County Wicklow

This charming village on the Shillelagh River was once in the midst of the great oak forests of Ireland which supplied the timbers for the roof of the medieval Westminster Hall. It also supplied timbers for the British Navy and for the roof of St Patrick's Cathedral in Dublin.

In the late 19th century the oak cudgel wielded by fighting tinkers was given the name 'Shillelagh', and the word became part of the Irish stage world of Victorian times so that today the distorted sticks of varnished blackthorn wood sold to tourists are called Irish 'Shillelaghs'.

SHILLELAGH is 22 miles south west of Wicklow town.

Inside Russborough House hang the priceless paintings collected by Sir Alfred Beit

Skerries is an ideal holiday destination with a good beach. It is also a sea-fishing centre

SKERRIES
County Dublin

From the Irish *Sceiri*, meaning sea rocks, Skerries is a charming seaside resort with a splendid harbour, a popular sailing club, a sandy strand and a good golf course. It was on St Patrick's Island, one and a half miles east of the village that St Patrick came ashore to get fresh water on his way from Wicklow up to Slemish in A.D. 432. You can see his footprint quite clearly in the rock. According to local legend the inhabitants of Skerries stole the Saint's goat and cooked and ate it while he was seeking fresh water. They became known as the 'skin the goats', and they do not take kindly to this story, so that when the architect of the local parish church put a statue of St Patrick with a goat at his feet at the entrance door, they had the goat chiselled off!

The other islands off the coast include Colt Island and Shenick's Island, and five miles out to sea stands Rockabill Lighthouse. Because of its historical association with St Patrick, Skerries was the setting for one of the most important of Synods A.D. 1148 and from this St Malachi was sent to Rome to seek the setting up of the first archbishops of Ireland. Hompatrick, at the southern end of the village, is the site of the monastery built by Sitric, the Norse King of Dublin, in 1120. There is a St Patrick's well in

Irish poet Francis Ledwidge was born in this cottage at Slane

undulating countryside of four counties, and as far as the sea. The monastic settlement and Round Tower of the 9th century was destroyed by Norse raiders. There are the remains of a 16th-century church on the site of the original church founded by St Patrick. From the west tower of these remains are magnificent views. The 9th-century monastic foundation here was associated with St Earc, first bishop of Slane.

Slane Castle, the seat of the Marquis of Conyngham, is a castelated mansion designed by the architect Francis Johnston, and set in a lovely demesne, and with a ballroom akin to the architecture of the Royal Pavilion in Brighton. George IV visited the castle twice, enamoured of the fat, fair, vulgar and avaricious Marchioness of Conyngham. He made her mistress of his household, and her husband was made his Lord Chamberlain.

In the village was born the poet Francis Ledwidge, 1887-1917, killed in action at Flanders.

SLANE is 29 miles north west of Dublin, 9 miles west of Drogheda.

SWORDS
County Dublin

Swords takes its name from the Irish *Sord Colaim Chille* meaning a pure well, blessed by St Columcille. He founded the monastery here which was run by St Finian the Leper. The monastic settlement was burnt and pillaged by the Norsemen on many occasions and the 75 ft high Round Tower would have been the safe refuge of the monastic treasures, books and chalices. A 14th-century square steeple was added to the Round Tower, and the present day ruins are all that remain of what was

the village, and a mile west is St Mobhi's Well, of the 7th-century saint who founded the monastery of Glasnevin in north Dublin. Two miles south are the magnificent ruins of the Norman castle of Baldongan. This was the 13th-century fortress home of the Barnewalls, then the Berminghams and then the St Lawrence family, Earls of Howth. Cromwell destroyed it in 1642 and butchered the garrison of 200. From the tower there is a fine view north of the Mountains of Mourne, and south to the Bay of Killiney.

SKERRIES is 19 miles north of Dublin city.

SLANE
County Meath

The village of Slane lies in the Boyne valley just a mile from the 529 ft high hill of Slane, where St Patrick lit the first Paschal Fire in Ireland in A.D. 433. The fire broke the blackout decreed by the pagan King Leary who witnessed it from the neighbouring Hill of Tara. With this fire St Patrick broke the power of the druids in Ireland and introduced Christianity. From the top of the hill are magnificent views of the once the country palace of the 13th and 14th-century Archbishops of Dublin.

🚗 *SWORDS is 8 miles north of Dublin City.*

TARA
County Meath

Tara — *Teamhair na Ríogh* — 'the Royal Acropolis' was the druidic and cultural capital of Ireland from time immemorial, the seat of pagan priest-kings and the centre of the national assembly for law making in peace and war. The pagan goddess Maeve was worshipped here and it became the seat of the High Kings of Tara. The last royal resident was Malachi II, High King of Ireland, who died in 1022. St Patrick came to Tara to confront the druids and convert the High King, Laoire. On the top of the hill is a modern statute of the saint and adjacent is the *Lia Fáil*, the Stone of Destiny, the coronation stone of ancient Kings. Royal palaces no longer stand on the site but there are grassy mounds marking the most historic of sites. The largest is the *Ráth na Ríogh*, the Royal Enclosure, 950 ft by 800 ft, in which stand the mound of King Cormac's House, and of the Royal Seat. Within the Royal Enclosure is the Grave Mound of the Hostages, dating from some 2000 years B.C. Cormac's house has defensive banks and ditches. South of the Royal Enclosure is the Ráth Laoghaire, and to the north is the three-ringed fort, the Ráth of the Synods. The long, deep hollow north of this with its high banks marks the site of the ancient Banqueting Hall which was 700 ft long and 90 ft wide. North west of the Banqueting Hall are the fort of Gráinne, King Cormac's daughter, the tragic lover of Diarmuid, and two other earthen mounds known as

Swords Church and round tower

the Sloping Trenches. On another hill, south of Tara, is the Ráth of Maeve, a hill fort some 750 ft in diameter. The songs of Thomas Moore, such as *The Harp That Once Through Tara's Halls*, have greatly glamourised what are now but mounds of earth, but, undoubtedly Tara is a place of enormous mystery spanning the times from pagan gods to St Patrick and the High Kings of Ireland.

🚗 *TARA lies 6 miles south of Navan and 23 miles from Dublin.*

WICKLOW
County Wicklow

The town of Wicklow sits snugly in the slopes of Ballyguile Hill on the mouth of the Vartry river, overlooking a wide crescent-shaped bay. Wicklow derives its name from the Danish *Wykinglo* — it was a Norse pirate station and slaving port. After the Norsemen the Normans took it over in the person of Maurice Fitz-Gerald. Then the local O'Toole and O'Byrne tribes fought over it. Maurice FitzGerald built the Black Castle, the ruins of which stand at the eastern end of the town on a rocky promontory. The Church of Ireland 13th-century church is built on the site of the medieval church of St Patrick and incorporates some of its 12th-century remains.

In the market square is a classic statue of a Wexford Pikeman of the Rebellion of 1798. He commemorates a bare-foot peasantry goaded into rebellion by the excesses of the Redcoats and German mercenaries who put down the Rebels with crack cavalry regiments and heavy artillery. From Wicklow Head, two miles south of the town, are magnificent views.

🚗 *WICKLOW is 32 miles south of Dublin.*

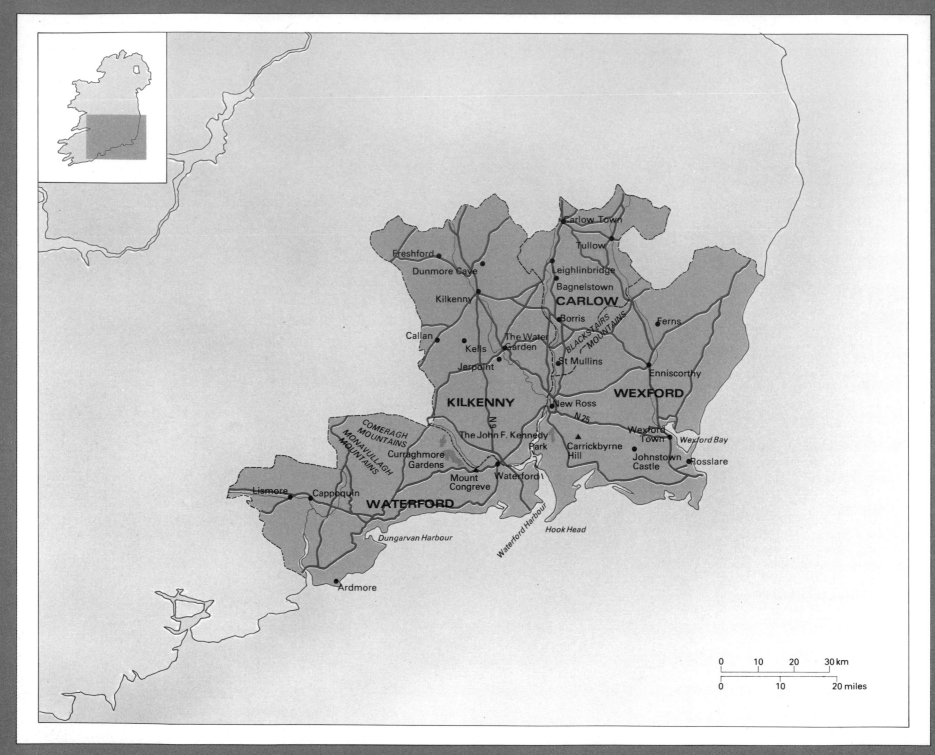

Carlow Town
Tullow
Freshford
Dunmore Cave
Leighlinbridge
Bagnelstown
Kilkenny
CARLOW
Borris
Ferns
Callan
The Water
Garden
Kells
BLACKSTAIRS MOUNTAINS
St Mullins
Jerpoint
Enniscorthy
WEXFORD
KILKENNY
New Ross
N 25
N 9
The John F. Kennedy
Park
Wexford
Town
Carrickbyrne
Hill
Wexford Bay
COMERAGH
MOUNTAINS
Curraghmore
Gardens
Johnstown
Castle
Rosslare
MONAVULLAGH
MOUNTAINS
Mount
Congreve
Waterford
Lismore
Cappoquin
WATERFORD
Hook Head
Dungarvan Harbour
Waterford Harbour
Ardmore

0   10   20   30 km
0   10   20 miles

The magnificent range of Comeragh mountains are a prominent part of the scenery of south east Ireland and can be seen for miles around

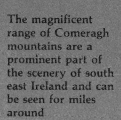OUNTY CARLOW, COVERING 346 square miles of rich, well watered, fertile farmland is only 29 square miles or so larger than Louth, Ireland's smallest county. This small but wealthy area can boast what is arguably the best provincial weekly newspaper in the country, *The Carlow Nationalist*, European in outlook. The sugar beet industry, flour milling, malting and a rich river, the Barrow, make it a fascinating and prosperous part of the country.

Kilkenny, historically the seat of the Butlers of Ormonde, the royal representatives of English kings, is today best known for its internationally famous Irish design centre, situated in the stables and coach houses of Kilkenny Castle, and the sport of hurling, which is played with

a vengeance in this part of the country.

The name of Waterford is, of course, synonymous with cut glass, an ancient Irish craft revived by the McGrath family. Wexford, another county, like Waterford, with a magnificent sea coast, is internationally renowned for its Festival of Opera. This successful annual event, which attracts enthusiasts and critics from all over Europe and America, was the brain-child of Dr Tom Walsh, founder of the festival, and his friend and colleague the late Eugene McCarthy, whose family still run the centuries-old White's Hotel in the town centre. The town, on the River Slaney, is of great antiquity and still bears signs of its Norman heritage.

ARDMORE
County Waterford

Ardmore, in addition to being an attractive seaside resort beautifully located on Ardmore Bay, has the remains of a superb monastic site of the 7th century, founded by St Declan, bishop of Munster before the arrival of St Patrick. These remains include a splendid Round Tower 97 ft high and divided into four storeys. St Declan's Oratory is a tiny church 14 ft long by 9 ft wide, with high pitched gables and a lintelled west door. It was re-roofed in 1716. The Cathedral dates from the 10th century. It has a well-proportioned nave and a chancel. The external wall of the West gable is quite remarkable, a Romanesque arcade of carved figures normally seen on Celtic High Crosses. The ruins also include the Hermitage Church, St Declan's Holy Well, and, on the beach, St Declan's Stone.

Ardmore is some 30 miles south west of Waterford.

BAGNELSTOWN
County Carlow

Bagnelstown, a charming town on the River Barrow, takes its name from Walter Bagnel, who had the grandiose idea of building an Irish version of Versailles on the site. Today the town has reverted to its old Irish name, *Muine Bheag*, 'The Little Shrubbery.' Walter Bagnel lived in Dunleckny Manor, north of the town. His ancestor, Sir Nicholas Bagenal, was a general in the army of Queen Elizabeth and was thus able to purchase vast estates in County Carlow in 1585. Two miles east of the town are the imposing ruins of the 14th-century Ballymoon Castle, a square enclosure with towers, built by the Carew family in

Ardmore church and round tower are sites of great antiquity

the tempestuous 13th century.

BAGNELSTOWN, or Muine Bheag, as it is signposted, is 11 miles from Carlow and 63 from Dublin.

BORRIS
County Carlow

Borris, also known as Borris Idrona, from its name in Irish, is a picturesque Georgian town in the east of the valley of the River Barrow. It is delightfully situated between the foot of the Blackstairs Mountains whose highest point is Mount Leinster, 2610 ft high, and the Hill of Brandon, great walking and climbing country.

Just west of the village itself is Borris House, home of the Mac Murrough Kavanaghs, direct descendants of the King of Leinster, Dermot Mac Murrough Kavanagh, who made possible the Norman occupation of the greater part of Ireland in the 1170s. Some say that due to this a curse was laid on the family, particularly the male heirs.

Be this as it may, the most remarkable and famous of the male Mac Murrough Kavanaghs was the one who lived from 1831 to 1889 and was born without arms or legs. Despite this he learned to ride a horse in a specially constructed saddle-seat, learned to shoot and became a Member of Parliament!

BORRIS is approximately 60 miles from Dublin.

CALLAN
County Kilkenny

Callan, from the Irish *Calainn*, Callan's Tribe, is a busy little town, medieval in origin, and older than Kilkenny as it received its Charter in 1271 from William the Marshal, who established a manor house there. In 1391 it was bought by James Butler, Earl of Ormonde. It

The smooth waters of the River Barrow flow through County Carlow

was a walled town in the 15th century, subject to attack by the local O'Carroll of Ely clan, and in 1650 it was surrendered to Cromwellian forces by Ormonde's governor Sir Robert Talbot. For a small town it has produced some remarkable people. James Hoban, the architect of the White House in Washington D.C. was born near Callan in 1762. Robert Fulton, who designed the first steamship the world ever saw was born in the town in 1765. In the main street is a memorial, a life-size statue, to Brother Edmund Rice, 1762-1844, the founder of the famous Irish educationalists, the Christian Brothers. He was born in the townland of Westcourt, adjacent to the town. The thatched farmhouse in which he was born has been preserved in its 18th-century form, and a chapel and a monastery has been built nearby. In the town are the ruins of the 15th-century Augustian Friary. It was founded by Eamonn MacRisdera Butler of Puttlerath in 1452. His son James built the rectangular church with its central tower. The chancel is near the local Church of Ireland parish church. James was the father of Sir Piaras Rua Butler, Earl of Ossory and Ormonde.

🚗 *CALLAN is 6 miles south west of Kilkenny.*

CAPPOQUIN
County Waterford

Cappoquin, *Ceapac Cuinn*, Conn's Plot of Land, is a beautiful and peaceful market town set in wooded countryside, at the foot of the glorious Knockmealdown Mountains, where the Glenshelan River joins the River Blackwater. Across the fine stone bridge, four miles to the north, is the Trappist Monastery of Mount Mellaray, founded by the

Cappoquin — a peaceful market town set in wooded countryside

CARRICKBYRNE HILL
County Wexford

At over 700 ft high Carrickbyrne Hill offers magnificent panoramic views of the surrounding countryside. It was an Insurgent encampment in the 1798 Rebellion for the period approaching the battle for New Ross. At nearby Carrigadaggin is a granite memorial, erected in 1841, to the memory of a very gallant English soldier, Sir Ralph Abercromby. He was commander-in-chief of the British forces in Ireland just prior to the 1798 Rebellion. He protested again and again in the strongest possible terms about the barbaric behaviour of the Redcoats, and in particular of the brutality of the Hessian forces, the German mercenary troops. Since the Government was bent on goading the peasants into revolt they forced him to resign his command.

CARRICKBYRNE is 8 miles south-east of New Ross.

CURRAGHMORE GARDENS
County Waterford

Curraghmore Gardens are beautifully landscaped grounds next to Curraghmore, the seat of the Marquis of Waterford. There is a shell house decorated in 1754 by Catherine, Countess of Tyrone. The selection of trees is magnificent, and in the months of May and June the rhododrendra, the azaleas and the bluebells are at their very best.

The House is open to groups by advance arrangement. The demesne of the Marquis of Waterford is 10 miles of high hills, deep valleys and rich oak forests through which the River Clodiagh flows.

CURRAGHMORE GARDENS are in the village of Portlaw, 10 miles from the city of Waterford.

Cistercians in 1832, who turned a barren mountainside into 800 acres of farmland and built a magnificent Abbey monastery, seminary and guesthouse. Renowned for its traditional hospitality, the guesthouse takes visitors free. The custom is for visitors or pilgrims to make any offering they think fit, although they are not strictly obliged to do so.

CAPPOQUIN is 131 miles south of Dublin and 4 miles from Lismore.

CARLOW TOWN
County Carlow

Carlow Town, from the Irish *Ceatarlac*, meaning the 'Fourfold Lake', beautifully situated on the River Barrow, is a prosperous modern town, once an Anglo-Norman fortress on the edge of the 'Pale', that area around Dublin which the Normans occupied, and beyond which they could not keep a military presence. In 1361 it was a walled city and remained so until the 1650s. When the peasants of Carlow rose in rebellion in 1798, the Redcoats killed 650 in the fighting, and today a beautiful Celtic Cross marks the grave of 400 rebels buried on one side of the town. Carlow Castle, built in 1200 by William le Mareschal, changed hands many times in many battles and its remains still stand near the bridge on the Barrow, once a rectangular building with a circular Norman tower, now reduced to two towers on the west bank. Cromwell captured it in 1650 and after that it was occupied by Donough, Earl of Thomond.

It became the property of a Dr Middleton, who in order to make room for the erection of a lunatic asylum, blew up part of the Castle in 1814! The Catholic Cathedral of the Assumption was built in 1833 and has a unique lantern tower 150 ft high. The Cathedral contains a superb marble monument to Bishop Doyle by the Irish sculptor Hogan. The Courthouse has a splendid granite Doric portico modelled on the Parthenon in Athens. Two miles east of Carlow at Browne's Hill, is a dolmen with the largest capstone in Europe. The dolmen dates from 2500 B.C., and its 100 ton capstone is balanced on the earth and three standing stones.

At Killeshin, three miles west of the town, are the ruins of Killeshin Church which include a splendid example of a Hiberno-Romanesque doorway.

CARLOW lies 52 miles south west of Dublin on an old coaching road with little traffic.

Fabulous Clonea Strand at Dungarvan is ideal for seaside holidays

DUNGARVAN
County Waterford

'Dun' is Irish for fortress, so it is hardly surprising that this lively town, with its thriving port, has two castles; Dungarvan Castle and Prince John's Castle in its environs.

Adopted by the Normans, Dungarvan now plays a large part in the great revival of the Gaelic language. People came from all over Europe to learn Gaelic on the nearby peninsula of *An Rinn*.

Dungarvan is ideally situated for those who wish to explore the nearby mountain ranges of Monavullagh and Comeragh.

DUNGARVAN is on the N25, 28 miles south-west of Waterford and 44 miles north-east of Cork.

DUNMORE CAVE
County Kilkenny

At Dunmore are the largest and most accessible limestone caves in the country, specially lit and equipped with a viewing balcony for

29

Ancient Dunmore Cave has played its part in Irish history. It is now specially lit and open to visitors

visitors. Dunmore comes from the Irish, *Derc Ferna*, the Cave of the Alders. In 928 the raiding Vikings put to death 1000 people who had sheltered there. The cave has a direct historical association with the legendary Kilkenny 'Cats', for it is recorded in the ancient Book of Leinster that a gigantic cat, known in Irish as *Luchthigern*, – the Lord of the Mice – lived in this cave. The interior of the limestone cave is shaped not unlike a recumbent cat with an outstretched tail. Stalagmites and dripstone formations abound.

DUNMORE CAVE is 7 miles north of Kilkenny.

ENNISCORTHY
County Wexford

Enniscorthy is a charming market town, perfectly placed in the middle of the county, in rich, agricultural land in the valley of the River Slaney. It is positioned on both sloping banks of the river, and spanned by a magnificent six-arched bridge. The Norman castle of Raymond le Gros was originally built here in 1235, and rebuilt in the 1590s by Sir Henry Wallop. This four-storey castle has rounded turrets and was associated with the Elizabethan poet, Edmund Spenser. The town is immortalised in the ballads of the 1798 Rebellion, as the rebels held it against the forces of General Lake for several weeks. Long before it went up in flames in 1798, it had been damaged in 1649 by the siege guns of Cromwell. In the market square are the statues of Father Murphy, the patriot priest leader of

This memorial to the 1798 Rebellion stands in Enniscorthy

1798, who was executed, and a pikeman. At the eastern edge of the town lies Vinegar Hill, 390 ft high, equally famous in patriotic songs and ballads, as it was here that the Insurgents made their last desperate stand against the superior forces of General Lake and General Johnson.

One of the most famous ballads, *The Boys of Wexford*, refers to the 'bold Shelmalier', with his long-barrelled gun, which was the duck hunting gun used by the fowlers of this area, who made such expert snipers in the Insurgent forces. Father John Murphy, the Insurgent leader, headed up his peasant forces armed with pikes after the Redcoats had burnt the Catholic church of Boolavogue, just north of Enniscorthy. This burning was the *causus belli* of the 1798 Rebellion. The ballad *Boolavogue* was a special favourite of the late U.S. President John F. Kennedy. The castle of Enniscorthy is now a folk museum.

ENNISCORTHY is 15 miles north west of Wexford.

FERNS
County Wexford

Ferns, *Fearna* – The Alder Trees – now a quiet and pleasant little village, was once the capital of the Province of Leinster and the episcopal see of the 6th century St Maodhóg, better known as St Aidan. The monastery he founded was repeatedly sacked by the Norsemen. Dermot Mac Murrough Kavanagh founded an Abbey here for the Canons Regular of St Augustine. It was burnt down in 1154, rebuilt in 1160 and given to the Augustinians. The ruins of the west tower, the north wall of a church, a sacristy and some of the cloisters remain. The church would have been barrel-vaulted like Cormac's Chapel at Cashel. Parts of the old church are incorporated in the present Church of Ireland building. The sculptured Celtic High Cross in the graveyard marks the grave of King Dermot, the greatest traitor in Irish history. He abducted his neighbour's wife, and then invited Henry II to invade Ireland, blessed by a bull given by Pope Adrian IV, the only English Pope in history. The castle of Ferns occupies the site of the residence of King Dermot. The castle was built in the 12th century by the Earl Marshall family. It is a splendid example of Norman-Irish architecture with three of the four round towers remaining, each 30 ft in diameter. The chapel is circular, covered by a carved vault. Some of the 13th-century trefoil headed windows remain. The Mac Murrough's held the castle in the 14th century and the Cromwellian General Sir Charles Coote captured it in 1649 and butchered the inhabitants of Ferns. Until recently it was in the possession of the O'Donovan family.

FERNS is 68 miles south of Dublin and 21 miles north west of Wexford.

FRESHFORD
County Kilkenny

Freshford, today a busy market town with an attractive square, was once the monastic settlement of the princely St Lachtain who founded his church here in 622. There was a time when his arm was preserved in a 12th-century shrine, and this shrine can now be seen in the National Museum in Kildare Street, Dublin. On the original site of St Lachtain's church a larger church was erected in 1100, and the present church was built in 1730. It incorporates in its west gable the 12th-century Romanesque doorway. There is a steep pointed arch over the ornately carved Hiberno-Romanesque porchway. On the innermost jamb of the door is an inscription which asks for prayers for the builders: *Gill Mu-Cholmóc O Cenncucáin* and for *Mathgamain O Ciarmeic* for whom the church was made.

FRESHFORD is 9 miles north west of Kilkenny.

JERPOINT
County Kilkenny

Jerpoint Abbey is one of the finest examples of a Cistercian monastery in Ireland. It was founded in 1158 for the Benedictine Order by the King of Ossory, Donagh Mac Gillapatrick, and was associated

31

Jerpoint Abbey — one of the best examples of a Cistercian monastery to be found in Ireland

with Fountains Abbey in Yorkshire. After the suppression of the monasteries the Earl of Ormonde acquired it. A typical Cistercian monastery in lay-out, it would have had a huge choir in the abbey, surmounted by a tower, with an adjacent cloister, chapter house, kitchen, rectory and dormitory. The older portion of the ruins are 12th century with Hiberno-Romanesque chancel and transepts and the square, central 15th-century tower has typical Irish battlements. There is a row of six pointed arches between the nave and the north aisle. Sculptured figures of knights and saints adorn the much-restored cloister. The tombs include those of the Walsh family and one of the Butler family of the 15th and 16th century. The tomb of Bishop Felix O'Dullany who died in 1202, shows him holding a crozier which

has been partly gnawed by a snake. *THE ABBEY is on the banks of the little River Eoir, approximately 11 miles south east of Kilkenny.*

THE JOHN F. KENNEDY PARK
County Wexford

The John F. Kennedy Memorial Park is dedicated to John Fitzgerald Kennedy, who was President of the United States of America from January 1961 to his assassination on 22 November 1963.

It was inspired by the visit he made to the land of his fathers in June 1963. One of the highlights of this visit was his 'home-coming' to the Kennedy homestead in Dunganstown, where his second cousin once removed, the 'Widow Ryan' sat him down to tea and Irish soda bread. The homestead

still stands. The park was opened by the Irish government in May 1968 with the generosity and co-operation of many Irish-Americans who made the project possible.

It is a delightful leisure park, beautifully laid out and landscaped and with facilities for education and research, on the slopes of Slieve Coilte, just behind the ancestral house of the Kennedys in Dunganstown. It embraces 620 acres of land, over a third of which is devoted to the cultivation of specimen plantlife. It is primarily an arboretum, but also has some 6000 specimens of shrubs amid a garden forest of trees from five continents.

From the summit of Slieve Coilte you can view the entire park and the counties of Wexford and Waterford, including the Saltee Islands, the estuary of the Rivers Barrow, Nore

and Suir, and the entire Comeragh range of mountains.

John F. Kennedy had a deep and abiding love of Ireland, and particularly of Wexford. His first visit to Ireland was in 1938, when his father, Joseph P. Kennedy was the United States Ambassador in London. On his second visit to Ireland in 1947 the young John F. Kennedy paid his first visit to the ancestral home in Dunganstown. As Senator Kennedy he visited Ireland in 1955 and was welcomed by the Irish Minister for External Affairs, Liam Cosgrave.

Wexford always retained a special place in his heart and on his inauguration day he had his favourite Irish Ballad of the Rebellion of 1798, *Boolavogue* sung for him.
THE JOHN F. KENNEDY PARK is 8 miles south east of the town of New Ross.

JOHNSTOWN CASTLE
County Wexford

Johnstown Castle was built in the 13th century by the Anglo-Norman family of Esmonde. Cromwell had the castle taken down, and a Cromwellian soldier sold it to John Grogan of Yorkshire in 1683. By coincidence the marriage of a widow, Mrs Grogan-Morgan to Sir Thomas Esmonde brought the castle back to its original owners in the 19th century. It then became the residence of Lady Maurice Fitzgerald who died in 1942, and in 1946 this beautiful 19th-century Gothic castle was presented to the nation by her grandson and is in use today as a State Agricultural College. The castle is used for occasional banquets and the gardens are open to the public.

South of Johnstown Castle are the 'English Baronies' of Forth and Bargy. This title applies to the area from Wexford Harbour to Bannon Bay. This Anglo-Norman countryside has many well-preserved castles, abbeys and churches. Until recently the people of the baronies spoke a dialect in which many early Anglo-Norman words were preserved. In 1169 Robert FitzStephen and Hervey de Marisco landed with 30 men in armour, 60 armoured horses, and 300 bowmen. Dermot MacMurrough, the traitor King of Leinster, joined the Norman freebooters with a force of Danes, and the combined forces took Wexford in the first battle for the Norman Conquest of Ireland.

JOHNSTOWN CASTLE is 5 miles south-west of Wexford town.

The grey turrets and landscaped gardens of Johnstown Castle in County Wexford

KELLS
County Carlow

The Augustinian Priory at Kells was founded in 1193 by Geoffrey de Marisco; Geoffrey FitzRobert de Monte de Marisco to give him his full title, Strongbow's strong-arm man for the Province of Leinster. This was established in the vicinity of an ancient monastic site of St Ciaran, as just two miles south at Kilree is a magnificent 96 ft high Round Tower and a Celtic cross which marks the burial place of Niale Caille, High King of Ireland.

The substantial ruins of the 14th and 15th centuries mark one of the largest collections of medieval buildings in Ireland. Originally the Augustinian Abbey covered five acres of land. The original Abbey or Priory consists of a nave and chancel topped by a huge square tower. There is an aisle to the west of the cruciform church with a Lady Chapel on the east side of the transept. The nave and choir form the cross piece of the cruciform and off the main body of the church is a square cloister and a huge kitchen. The tower at the north west of the main church would have been the residence of the Prior. South of the Priory was fortified by walls and five turrets. The monastery was suppressed in 1540 and granted to the Earl of Ormonde.

🚗 *KELLS is 6 miles from Callan and 10 miles from Kilkenny.*

KILKENNY
County Kilkenny

Kilkenny, a charming cathedral city of considerable prosperity and importance, standing on both banks of the River Nore, has attractive narrow winding medieval streets. Its name in Irish is *Cill Cainnig*, meaning 'Canice's Church', since it was founded by Saint Canice of Aghaboe in the 6th century. It was capital of

St Canice's Cathedral, built in the 13th century

Glowing stonework inside St Canice's Cathedral, Kilkenny

the Irish Kingdom of Ossory. In Anglo-Norman times the freebooter Strongbow built a castle near the monastery of St Canice to command the river crossing of the Nore. His son-in-law, William le Mareschal, inherited it and built it into a solid stone castle in 1204. After being in the hands of the de Clares and the Staffords it was bought by James Butler, 3rd Earl of Ormonde in 1391.

Kilkenny became the seat of many parliaments, and one, in 1366, established the Statutes of Kilkenny. These were enacted because the Anglo-Normans were becoming 'more Irish than the Irish themselves'. Thus the Normans were forbidden to marry the native Irish, adopt their dress or names or language, and all Irish monks and clerics were kept out of Norman monasteries and cathedrals. In the cathedral in 1575, Rory O'Moore, King of Laois, bowed the knee to Elizabeth. The foremost educationalists in Europe, the Jesuits, set up a school in 1619. From 1642 until 1648 the old Irish and the Anglo-Irish Catholics came together in the Assembly known as the Confederation of Kilkenny, which was virtually an Irish parliament. This was a glorious period for the city. Owen Roe O'Neill represented the Old Irish and the Anglo-Normans were represented by the English Viceroy, Ormonde, who in the event, sold the Confederation down the river, and it collapsed. General Owen Roe O'Neill died in 1649, and a year later Kilkenny fell to Cromwell, who, strangely enough, permitted the surrendered garrison to move out with full military honours. His troops 'utterly defaced and ruined' the Cathedral Church of St Canice by taking down the roof, removing all glass from the windows and stealing the doors and the five bells, 'so that hogs might come and root, and the dogs gnaw the bones of the dead.'

St Canice's Cathedral, a 13th-century building, stands on the site of the 6th-century monastic settlement of St Canice, and the 9th-century Round Tower still stands, 100 ft high, and affords a panoramic view of the city. The cathedral contains the finest collection of tombs of any church in Ireland. It includes the 1285 monument to the son of Henry de Ponto of Lyra, and the 1549 tomb of Edmund Purcell, who was a leader of Ormonde's Gallowglasses, the bodyguards of kings and princes who wielded double-headed axes. Another tomb is of the Franciscan Bishop, de Ledrede, who died in 1360, another to Bishop Rothe, of 1645. There is an altar tomb to the Bishop Hacket dated 1478.

The Black Abbey, in Abbey Street, is a Dominican church incorporating the building of 1225 by William le Mareschal, Earl of Pembroke. Not far away is St Canice's Well, with its stone well house. It has a strange history, for the 13th-century Bishop, Geoffrey de Turville, granted the friars the right to a supply of well water on condition that the water pipe did not exceed the diameter of his episcopal ring. The Black Freren Gate in Abbey Street is the only medieval gate remaining of the once walled city. There are also the ruins of St Francis Abbey of the Grey Friars.

In St Kieran's Street is Kyteler's Inn, Kilkenny's oldest house. Here the witch, Dame Alice Kyteler, was born in 1280, carried on a business as a money lender, became immensely wealthy and dabbled in sorcery. She was suspected of poisoning her four husbands, and in 1324 was tried and convicted of witchcraft. She escaped to England and

Kilkenny's streets retain an old-fashioned atmosphere

left her maid, Petronella, to be burnt at the stake.

The Magdelen Castle, situated in Maudlin Street, was once a medieval leper hospital. It is a square defence tower built to protect the barns and farmyard of the Earls of Ormonde. In Callan Road is St Kieran's College, the diocesan college of the Catholic diocese of Ossory. Among its famous professors were Francis Sheehy-Skeffington, the pacifist, shot in Dublin in 1916 on the orders of Captain Bowen-Colthurst, and the poet leader of the 1916 Insurrection, Thomas McDonagh who was executed by a firing squad.

The 13th-century Kilkenny Castle is the pride of the city. This was the residence of the Butler family, the Dukes of Ormonde. In the old stable of the Castle are the Kilkenny Design Workshops.

These workshops set standards of excellence of design for the whole country in crafts such as weaving, textile-printing, pottery and jewellery making. The original Kilkenny Design Shop has on sale some of the finest hand made crafts in the country. You can see silversmiths, potters and hand weavers at their work. Everything from furniture to candles to hand-blown crystal glass, stonewear and porcelain is on sale to the public, the products of some 35 small craft industries in all.

The Tholsel, now the City Hall, was once the tollhouse of the city, and was built in 1761. The records of the city dating back to 1230 are housed here, along with the city's historic sword and mace. Opposite Kilkenny Castle is Kilkenny College, a Georgian building of 1782. It is built on the site of the old college of St John built in 1616. Kilkenny College educated Swift (1667-1745), Congreve (1670-1729) Berkeley (1685-1753), Farquhar (1678-1707) and the novelist brothers, John Banim (1798-1842) and Michael Banim (1796-1874).

KILKENNY *is 73 miles south of Dublin, 30 miles north of Waterford.*

LEIGHLINBRIDGE
County Carlow

This pleasant village on the River Barrow once guarded a strategic bridge across the river. It is famous for its Black Castle, erected in 1180 by Hugh de Lacey. This was later the site of a 12th-century Carmelite monastery and the present castle was built in 1547 by Sir Edward Bellingham. Sir Peter Carew and the Bagenals also occupied it. The Kavanaghs and the Butlers and the O'Moores fought over it, and Colonel Hewson demolished it on behalf of Oliver Cromwell. Part of the 16th-century tower still remains, as do some defensive walls. The stone bridge over the river still incorporates stones of the original bridge built in 1320 by Maurice Jakis, a Canon of Kildare Cathedral who was a noted bridge builder.

At Cranavonane, in the parish of Leighlinbridge, in 1717 was born Edmund Cullen, the grandfather of Paul Cullen, Ireland's first Cardinal. Hugh Cullen, the Cardinal's father, was born in 1760. For his part in the Rising of 1798 he was imprisoned in Naas jail and other relatives were shot. Not surprisingly as this family was of Irish Jacobite patriot stock and as officers its members had fought in the Confederate army of 1641. Paul Cullen, the future Prince of the Church, was educated at Carlow College which gave sanctuary to 600 rebels in the battle for Carlow in 1798. Paul studied in Rome, became Rector of the Irish

College there and later Primate of All Ireland.

In May 1866 he became Ireland's first Cardinal, a confidant of Pope Pius IX, and revered by John Henry, later Cardinal Newman. He died on 24 October 1878. There is a statue of this lion of a man by Sir Thomas Farrell in the Catholic Pro-Cathedral in Dublin.

LEIGHLINBRIDGE is 7 miles south of Carlow town.

LISMORE
County Waterford

Lismore, sitting pretty on the south bank of the River Blackwater, was originally the site of the 7th-century monastic university city of St Carthach. St Colman, in the 8th century, presided over no less than 20 churches on this site. The Norsemen sacked it frequently and Henry II occupied it to receive the submission of the chiefs of Leinster and of Munster. Raymond le Gros destroyed the monastic city in 1173.

The sheer beauty of the setting of the village is reflected in the delicately poised Lismore Castle overhanging the Blackwater on a cliff. King John built it in 1185 on the site of St Carthach's monastery. It was once in the possession of Sir Walter Raleigh, and Richard Boyle possessed it in 1602, the 'Great' Earl of Cork. His son, Robert Boyle, the famous chemist, who gave his name to 'Boyle's Law' was born in the castle in 1755. It is now the property of the Duke of Devonshire and has the best salmon fishing waters in Ireland.

LISMORE is 134 miles from Dublin and 36 miles from Cork.

Beautiful Lismore Castle looks out over treetops and the dancing progress of the River Blackwater

Such is the reputation of Kilkenny for the generosity and prosperity of its people that a traditional rhyme says:
'Whenever you go to Kilkenny Just ask for the Hole-in-the-Wall, You'll get 24 eggs for a penny, And butter for nothing at all.'
Still prosperous today, the city is internationally known for its Kilkenny Design Workshops which have become the shop-window of Ireland. The studios are in the cleverly re-designed Kilkenny Castle stables and coach houses, built in the late 18th century by the Earl of Ormonde. The workshops are responsible to the government for raising the standards of design in industry and among consumers throughout the country. Behind the little-changed facade are modern workshops for all types of crafts including hand weaving, silverware, hand-thrown stoneware, prototypes of furniture and engineering products, fabrics, jewellery and porcelain. The Kilkenny shops provide VAT-free prices for purchases sent direct to tourist's homes and have a worldwide mail order business.

A panel of experts vigorously assesses and tests products from all over Ireland for value, quality and design. There is also a branch shop in Dublin.

Kilkenny Design Centre

Inside Kilkenny Castle the craftsmen perfect their designs

College and Trinity College, Dublin, his best known drama being the comedy *The Way of the World* (1700). Another William Congreve invented matches, and the first rockets used as weapons, used by the Royal Navy at the battle of Copenhagen, and it was Ambrose Congreve who was responsible for today's woodland garden and vast walled enclosure of lawns and herbaceous borders.

Plants include some hydrangea and buddleia, Oriental poppies, rhododendra, rare plants from South America and Tasmania, and magnolia trees of spectacular beauty. Expert gardeners reckon it to be one of the glories of Ireland, and its high terraces and walks above the beautiful River Suir give it a perfect setting.

MOUNT CONGREVE demesne is 4 miles west of the town of Portlaw, which is 9 miles west of Waterford.

NEW ROSS
County Wexford

Delightfully placed on a hillside above the River Barrow, New Ross, one of Wexford's oldest towns, has narrow, winding streets. It was built on the site of the 6th-century monastery of St Abban, a walled town which did not surrender to a fierce siege by the Duke of Ormonde. Cromwell captured it in 1649, and in 1798 it was held briefly by the Insurgent forces under their leader Bagenal Harvey. Today, a trip aboard the *New Ross Galley* offers a splendid opportunity to see the beauty of the surrounding countryside from five miles of river whilst wining and dining.

Five miles from New Ross is the National Memorial Park and Arboretum, dedicated to the memory of U.S. President John F. Kennedy.

MOUNT CONGREVE
County Waterford

The gardens of Mount Congreve, on the south bank of the River Suir, have been described as 'one of the grandest woodland gardens in Europe' and 'one of the very few Irish gardens in which planting of flowering trees and shrubs still continues on a lavish scale.'

The Georgian house on the demesne was built by John Congreve in 1725. Not only were members of the family world-renowned gardeners but they included the dramatist William Congreve (1670-1729), a contemporary of Swift at Kilkenny

At Dunganstown, near New Ross, is the cottage in which the great-grandfather of President Kennedy was born.

🚗 *NEW ROSS is 27 miles south east of Kilkenny.*

ROSSLARE
County Wexford

Rosslare – the Middle Peninsular – with six miles of curving, sandy beach, has the unique reputation of being the driest and sunniest place in Ireland. The harbour is the terminal for car ferries from Fishguard and Le Havre. Just off the coast is the Tuskar Rock with its famous lighthouse, erected in 1815, and whose beams are visible for more than 20 miles in the busy sea lanes. South of Rosslare harbour is Carnsore Point where there are the remains of an ancient church and the Holy Well of St Vaux, an Irish saint who died in Brittany in A.D. 585. The sandy beach of Carne once appeared on Ptolemy's 2nd-century map of the then-known world as *Hieron Akron*, the Holy Cape. A few miles off the coast are the Saltee Islands, a sanctuary for over three million wild birds in spring and summer.

🚗 *ROSSLARE is 11 miles south east of Wexford.*

ST MULLINS
County Carlow

Carlow's claim to monastic fame lies in St Mullins, the foundation of St Moling who died in 698. Here the Saint achieved the impossible by persuading the men of Leinster to let the men of Munster off the 'Borama', the tribute of cattle which they had been obliged to pay. The McMurrough-Kavanaghs, Kings of

New Ross, on the River Barrow, is one of County Wexford's oldest towns

Leinster, lie buried here. St Moling was Bishop of Glendalough, and of Ferns. His Abbey is medieval with an unusual spiral staircase. There are the remains of what was once a Round Tower, St Jame's Chapel, and a Celtic High Cross of granite featuring the crucifixion. There are also the remains of some Norman buildings. The Norsemen plundered the monastery in 951 and in 1138 almost razed it to the ground. Ancient 7th-century manuscripts describe the original plan of the monastery in considerable detail.

ST MULLINS *is 9 miles south of Borris, in the Barrow Valley, and 79 miles south of Dublin.*

TRAMORE
County Waterford

This splendid seaside resort counts golden sands, a miniature railway and a boating lake among its many attractions. Those who enjoy a flutter at the races will have heard of Tramore's famous racecourse.

Quite apart from these modern day features, archaeologists will find a great deal to interest them in the vicinity as earthworks, passage graves and castles abound.

TRAMORE *is 8½ miles south of Waterford and 23 miles east of Dungarvan on the coast road.*

TULLOW
County Carlow

The neat market town of Tullow was once the setting for a Butler castle which commanded the river crossing, and the garrison of a subsequent castle fell to Cromwell's forces in 1650, and were put to the sword. Richard II's hirelings took the surrender of the King of Leinster, Art MacMurrough in 1395 in a meadow near Tullow. By this submission, Art and his followers left the province of Leinster. In the market square is a splendid statue of Father John Murphy, the insurgent leader of the 1798 Rebellion who was hanged in the town.

Tramore's glorious golden sands and good amenities make it an ideal holiday resort

Some four miles east of the town is the traditional burial place of the Kings of Leinster, the ancient four ring stone hillfort of Rathgall. It is 1000 ft in diameter and covers 18 acres. The central fort is 150 ft in diameter with an 18 ft thick rampart. At Aghade, a few miles south of Tullow is the *Cloch and Phoill*, the Holed Stone, a large, flat leaning stone with a hole half a foot wide at one end. In mythology it is the stone to which Niall of the Nine Hostages tied Eochaidh, son of Enna Cinnselach by a chain. He snapped the chain and slew all nine of the men Niall had sent to kill him. This area has a number of grooved standing stones, pre-historic graves and portal dolmens and bronze age cemeteries.

TULLOW is 50 miles south of Dublin.

WATERFORD
County Waterford

The ancient city of Waterford, perched on the south side of the noble River Suir, has a fine harbour on the confluence of the rivers Nore and Barrow. 'Waterford' is a Norse name *Vadrefjord*, which means that the marauding pirates stayed around long enough to name it after they arrived in A.D. 853. The Anglo-Normans under Strongbow and Raymond le Gros then took it. As was the Norman custom, the freebooter Strongbow consolidated his gain by marrying Eva, daughter of Dermot MacMurrough, the treacherous high king of Leinster, who had invited him to Ireland in the first place. Historians differ about the arrival in Waterford in 1171 of King Henry II, armed with a Papal Bull from the first and last ever English Pope, to 'convert' the Irish to Rome. So loyal were the citizens of Waterford to the crown that both King John in 1210

A craftsman at work on Waterford's best known export; beautiful hand-made glass

and Richard II in 1394 visited the city. Henry VII gave it its city arms, which remain today, *Urbs Intacta Manet Waterfordia*.

The Waterford Glass factory, which revived the 18th-century art of glass-blowing, is a mile or so down the road to Cork from Waterford City. The public can see the hand-made glass being created at set times each day. The glass itself is on sale in all the major stores and shops in the city and elsewhere in Ireland. The most striking building in Waterford is Reginald's Tower, a circular fortress with walls 10 ft thick, established by the Danes and taken

over by the Normans. There are still traces of the walls of the old Danish Norman city. Because of its sturdy people and able defences, Waterford is one of the few cities in Ireland which did not succumb to the butchery of Cromwellian troops. Cromwell besieged it, and had to retire, and in August 1650 his son-in-law, General Ireton took it and accepted an honourable surrender. The poet Spenser knew Waterford and wrote:

"...the gentle Shure that making way
By sweet Clonmell, adornes rich Waterford",

Reginald's Tower was erected by the

Danes in 1003 to defend the city, and Strongbow took it in 1171. King John turned it into a mint after he had imprisoned Fitzstephen there.

Near to the tower is the 'French Church' of the Grey Friars, originally a Franciscan church built in A.D. 1240 by Sir Hugh Purcell and much favoured by Henry III. When the monastery was suppressed in the course of the 16th-century Reformation it was bought, in 1545, by Patrick Walsh, who turned it into a hospital for the aged. Later, Huguenot refugees used it as a parish church, hence its name 'The French Church'. The City Hall, near

Reginald's Tower, was built in 1788 by John Roberts (1749-94), Waterford born, and great-grandfather of Field Marshal Lord Roberts. The council chamber boasts a genuine 18th-century chandelier of old Waterford Glass. Christchurch Cathedral, (18th century), was built on the site of a Danish church of A.D. 1050, replaced by architect John Roberts by another church in the 1770s. In Arundel Square are the remains of the Dominican church of 1226. In John's Lane, near the pre-sent St John's Catholic Church, are the remains of a Benedictine Priory of St John which was allied to the Benedictine Abbey of Bath. In the comparatively unknown church of the Dominicans in Bridge Street, is a 17th-century oak wood statue of 'Our Lady of Waterford'.

With the exception of Dublin, no other city in Ireland has produced such a variety of famous sons. They include Luke Wadding, the distinguished 16th-century Irish Franciscan historian, the great Shakespearean actor, Charles Kean (1811-1868); Vincent Wallace (1813-1865), composer of the opera *Maritana*; Thomas Francis Meagher, 'Meagher of the Sword' (1823-1867), the Young Ireland leader who led the Irish Brigade at the battle of Fredericksburg in the American Civil War, and who later became Governor of Montana; General Lord Roberts (1832-1914), 'Bobs', the most popular general in the army of Queen Victoria during the Boer War, and John Redmond, who represented the city as an M.P. for 25 years and was the last leader of the Irish Parliamentary Group at Westminster.

WATERFORD is 103 miles south of Dublin, 30 miles from Kilkenny and 39 miles from Wexford.

The city of Waterford straddles the banks of the River Suir. There is so much to see and do here visitors are spoilt for choice

THE WATER GARDEN
County Kilkenny

The Water Garden, at Ladywell, Thomastown, open to the public in the summer, is two acres of man-made aquatic heaven, complete with trees, shrubs and blooms which are at their best in the months of June and July. It is a restful place and teas can be taken on the terrace.

THE WATER GARDEN in Thomastown is 9 miles south of the city of Kilkenny.

WEXFORD TOWN
County Wexford

Wexford Town, on the River Slaney, was put on the world map by Ptolemy, the Greek geographer, in the second century A.D. He called it *Menapia*, after the Belgic tribe, the Menapi, who had settled on the site of present day Wexford before the time of Christ. It was captured by the Norsemen in the 9th century, and they called it *Waesfjord*, meaning 'the harbour of the mud flats'. The Norsemen settled down for 200 years and then the Norman free-booters led by Robert Fitzstephen, and with the treacherous connivance of Dermot MacMurrough, King of Leinster, landed and took over in 1169. In 1649 Oliver Cromwell captured the town and butchered all the inhabitants. For one month, in the Rebellion of 1798, it was held by the insurgent peasants against the Red-coats.

While Ptolemy was the first to put this coastal harbour town on the world map, Dr Tom Walsh of the local hospital brought Wexford to the forefront of international song when he established the annual Wexford Festival of Opera in 1951. The 'founding fathers' of this venture

The 'father' of the U.S. navy gazes out to sea at Wexford

were Tom Walsh, Eugene McCarthy, the owner of White's Hotel, Seamus O'Dwyer the local postman, Dr Desmond Ffrench, with Sir Compton Mackenzie as President. The first opera to be performed was *The Rose of Castile*, by the Irish composer, Michael William Balfe, who was born in Dublin in 1808. The present Church of Ireland, the church of St Selskar, occupies the site of the old 12th-century Abbey, of which the ancient tower remains. Early Irish Bishops such as Ó Aodha and Ó Maolaoidh, Bishops of Ferns, and some Norman bishops are buried here. The ruins of the Abbey near the Westgate Tower include the one remaining gateway out of the original five in the town walls. Henry II spent Lent in the Abbey in 1172 doing penance for the murder of Thomas a Becket. In 1175, Raymond le Gros married Strongbow's daughter Basilia there. In the Bull Ring stands a bronze statue of a Wexford Pikeman of 1798, the work of Oliver Sheppard of the Royal Hibernian Academy. No. 29 South Main Street was occupied by Oliver Cromwell. In North Main Street, now part of White's Hotel, was the old rectory where Sir Robert McClure was born, the arctic explorer and discoverer of the North West Passage.

On the seafront at Crescent Quay, is the statue of Commodore John Barry, founder of the American Navy. He was born at Ballysamson, Tacumshane, some ten miles from the town.

Three miles from the town is the Wexford Wildfowl Reserve, where half the population of Greenland's white fronted geese winter each year along with thousands of species of wildfowl.

WEXFORD is 88 miles south of Dublin.

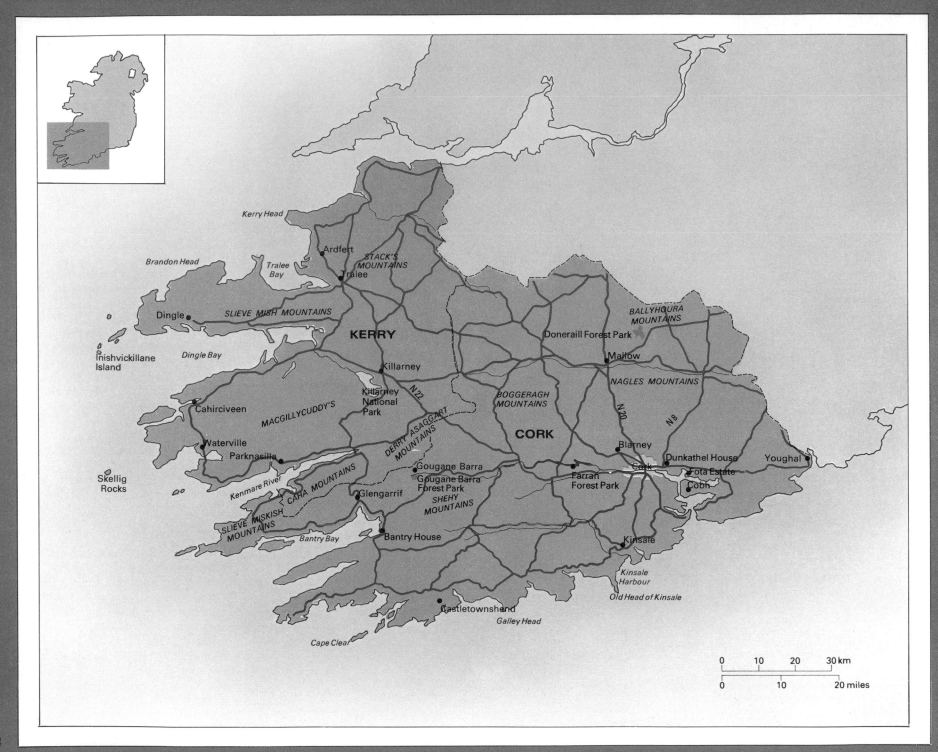

Kerry Head

Brandon Head

Tralee Bay

Ardfert

STACK'S MOUNTAINS

Tralee

Dingle

SLIEVE MISH MOUNTAINS

KERRY

BALLYHOURA MOUNTAINS

Doneraill Forest Park

Inishvickillane Island

Dingle Bay

Killarney

Mallow

Killarney National Park

N22

NAGLES MOUNTAINS

Cahirciveen

MACGILLYCUDDY'S

BOGGERAGH MOUNTAINS

N20

N8

Waterville

Parknasilla

DERRY ASAGGART MOUNTAINS

CORK

Blarney

Dunkathel House

Youghal

Skellig Rocks

Gougane Barra

Gougane Barra Forest Park

Farran Forest Park

Cork

Fota Estate

Kenmare River

CAHA MOUNTAINS

Glengarrif

SHEHY MOUNTAINS

Cobh

SLIEVE MISKISH MOUNTAINS

Bantry Bay

Bantry House

Kinsale

Kinsale Harbour

Old Head of Kinsale

Castletownshend

Galley Head

Cape Clear

| 0 | 10 | 20 | 30 km |

| 0 | 10 | 20 miles |

The golden spires of St Finbarr's Cathedral rise into the night sky amid the twinkling lights of Cork city

CORK AND KERRY are two counties in Ireland about which writers are prone to speak in superlatives. Cork, all 2880 square miles of it, is most famous for its Blarney Stone and its power of conferring the gift of eloquence on all who kiss it, or kiss it by proxy! To the east of Cork is rich river land with picturesque valleys. To the west, its mountains form mass ranks with the mighty mountain ranges of Kerry. The coast faces Spain, and points long fingers of land into the Atlantic. Around Glengarriff the land is lush, with a mediterranean climate caused by the warm waters of the Gulf Stream. The central valleys of the Blackwater, and of the River Lee are of quiet beauty. The 'Kingdom' of Kerry is a riot of high mountains, including the highest mountain in Ireland, Carrantuohill (3414 ft) and the land which embraces 'Heaven's Reflex', Killarney. Kerry is rugged Atlantic fjord coast, the next parish America. It was from Mount Brandon, 'Brendan's Mountain', that Brendan, the navigator Saint, set off in his frail craft, with his monk companions, and, sailing via Greenland and Iceland discovered America in the 6th century.

Cork is the glamour county, with a capital city which celebrated the 800th anniversary of its charter of foundation in 1985. Kerry is the romantic county, and both are rebels, far removed historically from the constraints of central government run from Dublin. Both retain their Irishry and independence of spirit.

Roofless Ardfert Cathedral stands in County Kerry

ARDFERT
County Kerry

Ardfert was a 6th-century monastic foundation of St Brendan the Navigator, who died in 577. In the 12th century it became the see of the diocese of Ardfert, and the cathedral was built. A 9th-century Round Tower from the original monastic settlement stood in the north-west corner of the church but was demolished by a great storm in 1771. The 12th-century nave and chancel church has a remarkable Hiberno-Romanesque doorway and on the walls of the cathedral ruins is a carving in stone of Bishop Stack who died in 1488. The choir is lit by a high three-light east window. Near the west end of the church are the remains of *Teampall na n-Oigh*, a Romanesque nave cum chancel church, and *Teampall Griffin*, a 15th-century church, which has a carved stone with a dragon and griffin inscribed on it, representing evil devouring itself. Ardfert Abbey, a Franciscan Friary, founded in 1253 by Thomas Fitzmaurice, the first Baron of Kerry, is just half a mile away.

One mile west of Ardfert is an early historic earthen fort where Sir Roger Casement (1864-1916) was captured after landing from a German submarine which had escorted the arms ship the *Aud*, bringing arms for the 1916 Rising. On Banna strand is a memorial commemorating the landing, the scuttling of the arms ship, and the arrest and execution of Casement.

ARDFERT is 5½ miles north west of Tralee.

BANTRY HOUSE
County Cork

The elegant home of the Egerton Shelswell-White family, and once the seat of the Earls of Bantry, from whom the family is descended, Bantry House is a treasure house of furniture, paintings, tapestries and objets d'art collected from all over Europe by the second Earl. It was built in 1750, and the magnificent south front was added to the original Georgian building in 1840. Open to the public it has refreshments and a craft shop.

BANTRY HOUSE is 56 miles west of Cork city and overlooks Bantry Bay.

CAHIRCIVEEN
County Kerry

Cahirciveen is a Y-shaped village nestling at the foot of Bentee Mountain (1245 ft high) beside the River Valentia, and overlooking Valentia harbour. A short distance from the town, on the road to Killorglin, are the ruins of Carhan House, where the Liberator, Daniel O'Connell was born in 1775. In the main street of the town is the massive Daniel O'Connell Memorial Church, built in 1888 from subscriptions by Kerry people from all over the world. On the western edge of the town is the Valentia weather observatory, one of the most important weather stations on the western seaboard of Europe. Across the water is the ancient Stone Fort of Cahergal, enclosed by a circular defence wall 14 ft thick and 79 ft in diameter. A little further north is the 9th-century Fort of Leacanabuaile. Valentia island, at the mouth of the river, was famous as the site of the Western Union Cable Station where the Atlantic cable on the bed of the sea joined telegraphic communications between the Old World and the New before the days of satellite communications. Ten miles south of Cahirciveen is the Stone Fort of Staigue, one of the finest pre-Christian stone forts in Ireland, with a massive stone wall 18 ft high, 13 ft thick and 90 ft in diameter. On the coast road to Staigue Fort from Cahirciveen is Derrynane House and National Park, the home of Daniel O'Connell, and now an excellent museum.

🚗 *CAHIRCIVEEN is 40 miles from Killarney, and 226 miles from Dublin.*

CASTLETOWNSHEND
County Cork

Castletownshend is one of the most attractive, secluded and safe sailing harbours in the county. It was the birthplace of Mrs George Bernard Shaw, and, at the entry to the village in Drishane House, lived Edith Oenone Somerville, (1858-1949), joint author with her cousin Violet Martin (1862-1915) of the classic *Experiences of an Irish R.M.* On the approach to the village is the 420 ft high hill of Knockdrum, an ancient stone ring fort with three finger stones still standing. At the foot of the steeply hilled village is the church of St Barrahane, and in its graveyard are the simple plain single stone graves of Dr Somerville and Violet Martin. The church is a gem with a Harry Clarke (1889-1931) stained glass south window to the memory of Sir Egerton Coghill, and an east window to the memory of the Somervilles. A third Harry Clarke window is to the memory of Colonel Coghill, a veteran of the Indian Mutiny. There is a superb Powell of London window dedicated to Lt. Nevill Coghill V.C. who died saving his regimental colours from the Zulus. The Celtic floor mosaics were designed by Dr Somerville. A mile from the church is the O'Driscoll fortress, Glenbarrahane Castle, occupied by a Spanish naval force in 1601, part of their expeditionary force for Kinsale. The Spanish naval forces successfully fought off the ships of Admiral Sir Richard Leveson.

🚗 *CASTLETOWNSHEND is 5 miles south of Skibbereen.*

COBH
County Cork

Cobh, pronounced 'Cove', was formerly known as Queenstown in honour of Queen Victoria's visit to Ireland in 1849. It stands at the enormous mouth of the River Lee, and was once a famous port of call for transatlantic liners. On the quayside is a memorial to those who died in the sinking of the *Lusitania* in World War I, by the Irish sculptor, Jerome Conor. In the Old Church cemetery are the graves of hundreds of the drowned. The town is dominated by St Colman's Cathedral, built by Pugin in 1868, with its glorious carillon of 47 bells.

It was from the former British naval dockyard at Rushbrooke that the *Sirius*, the first steamer to cross

Young sailors can pursue their hobby in Castletownshend's safe harbour

47

the Atlantic, sailed in April 1838. The King Alfred Royal Cork Yacht Club at Cobh, founded in 1720, is the oldest yacht club in the world.

● *COBH is 15 miles south east of Cork city.*

CORK
County Cork

Cork city derives its name from the Irish *Corach*, meaning 'A Marshy Place'. Ireland's third largest city, it was given its first charter by King Henry II of England in 1185. It was founded in the 6th century by St Finbarr, who set up his church and college on the south bank of the River Lee, where the present day University College stands. St Finbarr's small college prospered, and Cork developed into a university city throughout the 8th and 9th centuries. The Norsemen, nosing up the rivers of Ireland in their long boats, on hit and run raids, discovered Cork on the River Lee, and burnt it to the ground in A.D. 820. Eventually they settled, and the Danes lined up with the native Irish under the chieftain, Dermot MacCarthy. The wily Normans gave MacCarthy a Norman wife, and he then submitted to Henry II who granted the city its first charter. Predictably, the Normans soon became more Irish than the Irish themselves, and Cork prospered. In 1492 its people supported the Pretender to the throne of England, Perkin Warbeck. He and his supporters were hung at Tyburn. Then Cork supported Charles I until Cromwell put them down in 1649. Then Winston Churchill's ancestor, John Churchill, later to become the Duke of Marlborough, laid siege to the city for five days, demolished the walls with his artillery, and treated the surrendering citizens with honour. 'Rebel' Cork took a very active part in the War of Independence from 1919 to 1921.

St Colman's Cathedral seen above the serried ranks of houses at Cobh on the River Lee

A distinctly mediterranean atmosphere exists in Cork's attractive streets

This mediterranean style city has a unique pepper pot steeple, 120 ft high, in Shandon church, perched above the historic butter markets. Built in 1722, it has four different faces and chimes of eight bells. About these a local writer, Father Prout, wrote his poem with the opening lines,

"The Bells of Shandon,
that sound so grand on,
The pleasant waters of
the River Lee".

The mortal remains of Father Francis O'Mahoney (Father Prout) lie buried in the cemetery beside the church of St Anne, Shandon.

The Church of Ireland modern 'Gothic' church of St Finbarr ('The Fair Headed'), is on the site of a 6th century church set up by the monk who died in A.D. 623. All that remains of the medieval church on this site is a finely carved doorway. In the medieval church Edmund Spenser, the Elizabethan poet, married Elizabeth Boyle, daughter of the Earl of Cork. Spenser immortalised

The rooftops and spires of Cork, Ireland's third-largest city, rise out of the morning mist

this marriage in his ode, *Epithalamion*. Bishop Lyon, who performed the ceremony, lies buried just behind the high altar of the present church.

A peculiar feature of the modern Gothic St Finbarr's is a cannon ball suspended on a chain in the modern ambulatory. This 24 pound shot was fired from an Elizabethan cannon in the siege of the city in 1690, and was discovered embedded in the steeple of the cathedral when it was being demolished in 1865. A unique brass tablet in the cathedral reads:

"In pious memory of the Honourable Elizabeth Aldworth, wife of Richard Aldworth, of Newmarket Court, County Cork, Esq., daughter of Arthur, first Viscount Doneraile. Her remains lie close to this spot. Born 1695, Died 1775. Initiated into Freemasonry in Lodge No. 44, at Doneraile Court in this County A.D. 1712."

Apparently Elizabeth Aldworth was either hiding behind a screen or up the chimney of Doneraile Court, and overheard the masonic proceedings of Lodge No. 44, so she was made the only female Mason in history!

The city's southern residential suburb boasts a unique modern church, Christ the King, at Turner's Cross, by the Chicago architect, Barry Byrne. The Honan chapel, Donovan's Road, in the grounds of University College Cork, has what is arguably the most beautiful chapel in Ireland. It was built by the late Miss Belle Honan. It has a series of priceless modern Irish stained glass windows by Sarah Purser and Harry Clarke, built in 1916. Cork city has an excellent art gallery in Emmet Place, part of the Crawford Municipal School of Art.

St Patrick's Street is the principal street of the city, adorned by Foley's bronze statue of an apostle of temperance, the Capuchin Father Matthew. Cynics say he is pointing to the pub across the road! The South Mall is the commercial heart of the city and the Grand Parade has pleasant bow windowed houses.

A superb example of 18th-century architecture is Riverstown House, Glanmire, four and a half miles out of the city, on the Dublin road. It was built in 1602, and was the home of Dr Jemmett Browne, Bishop of Cork, who rebuilt it in 1745, and had the Francini brothers do the plaster work. The pleasant environs of Cork city include the Mardyke and Sunday's Well, and Montenotte, and Tivoli. Sir Walter Raleigh resided in Tivoli House, and Woodhill House was the residence of Sarah Curran, betrothed of Ireland's best loved patriot, Robert Emmet, who was hanged in Dublin for his quixotic Rising of 1803. His tragic romance inspired Moore to write one of his haunting melodies, *She is Far from the Land.*

Cork city has the reputation of providing much of the brains of the nation and has produced a number of talented literary figures. One of the best of romantic descriptive writers was D.L. Kelleher, who gave the Irish Tourist Board its slogan, 'Ireland of the Welcomes'. Of the stature of Turgenev and Chekov are the writers 'Frank O'Connor' (Michael O'Donovan) the short story teller, and the novelist and writer Sean O'Faolainn. Both were pupils of the novelist and Professor of Cork University, Daniel Corkery. In the visual arts Cork has produced Royal Academicians such as James Barry (1741-1806) and Daniel Maclise (1806-1870).

CORK city is 161 miles south west of Dublin, 61 miles from Limerick and 54 miles south east of Killarney.

The Blarney Stone

Blarney – *An Blarna* – meaning 'The Plain', is a pretty village north east of Cork, in which stands the massive castle, built in 1446, by Cormac MacCarthy to command the countryside known as Muskerry. It is four storeys high, and set in its topmost battlements is the magical Blarney Stone. With the aid of a guide you lie on your back, grasp iron safety rails, tip yourself, head first, backwards, and slip downwards, to kiss the stone. Legend has it that this will give you the gift of eloquence! The word 'Blarney' was introduced into the English language in 1602, by Queen Elizabeth I. Despite her repeated commands, her Deputy in Ireland, Lord Carew, had failed to bring to heel the wily chieftain of Muskerry, Cormac MacCarthy, who in order not to lose his elected position as clan chieftain, kept putting off his oath of allegiance to the Virgin Queen, by which he would acknowledge the lands belonged to her.

He gave Carew promises and half-promises, but never quite got round to bowing the knee. Finally, Her Majesty exploded with rage at Deputy Lord Carew's ineptitude and declared that the honeyed words and eloquent promises of the Irish Chieftain were all 'Blarney'.

Cormac's ploy paid off, as the castle remained outside the control of the Crown, and successfully withstood successive Cromwellian sieges.

Blarney castle is on the itinerary of most visitors to Ireland

To inherit the 'gift of the gab' you adopt this uncomfortable position

Beautiful Sybil Head on the Dingle Peninsula

Dingle's Gallerus Oratory is a well-preserved early stone building

DINGLE
County Kerry

Dingle – *Daingean ní Cúis* – the Fortress of O'Cush, is the most westerly town in Europe in an Irish-speaking area which has long historic links with Spain and France. It is bounded by hills on three sides, culminating in the north with the 3127 ft high Mount Brandon. A fishing port, it boasts at the corner of Main Street and Green Street the site of what was 'The Highest House in Dingle', once owned by a Colonel Rice of the Irish Brigade in France, who planned to rescue Marie Antoinette and bring her here. She refused to go when she learnt that the King and her children would have had to be left behind.

Across the harbour, is Burnham House, once the home of the local landlord, Lord Ventry. Ventry harbour, a few miles west, was the scene for a romantic 19th-century narrative poem discovered in the Bodlean Library, which relates that Dairre Donn, King of the World, was defeated here by the *Fianna* led by Fiona Mac Cumhaill, when he and his armies attempted to invade Ireland.

Slea Head a few miles to the west, is the nearest point on mainland Ireland to America. Offshore are the seven famous Blasket Islands. West Dingle is an archaeological paradise. The Fahan Group includes 414 clochans, or unmortared beehive-shaped cells, 19 souterrains, 18 standing stones, 2 sculptured crosses, 7 earthen forts and 2 fortified headlands. The forts include Dunbeg fort, Cathair Murphy, Cathair na Mairtineach and Cathair an Da Dhoras.

One of the most remarkable stone dwellings in the Dingle Peninsula is Gallerus Oratory, one of the most perfectly preserved Christian buildings in Ireland. Shaped like an upturned boat it is 22 ft long, 18 ft wide and 12 ft high. The entrance door is of the earliest Irish Christian architecture. It has stood for 1000 years, watertight, built throughout of unmortared stone.

DINGLE can be reached either by the coast road or across the spectacular 1500 ft high Connor Pass. The town is 42 miles west of Killarney and 31 miles south west of Tralee.

DONERAILE FOREST PARK
County Cork

Doneraile Forest Park is one of the latest acquisitions of the nation and is therefore not as widely known as it deserves to be.

It is the walled demesne of the former St Leger estate, 395 acres of rich rolling landscape abounding with deer.

Doneraile Court, a magnificent three-storey mansion, is leased to the Georgian Society of Ireland. It was built in 1725 and reached its present proportions in the early 1900s. The Duke of Atholl planted the first European Larch trees on the lawn in front of the house in 1738.

DONERAILE PARK is 6 miles north-east of Mallow.

DUNKATHEL HOUSE
County Cork

Dunkathel House, little known, is the splendid 18th-century mansion of Mr & Mrs Geoffrey Russell, built in the architectural style of David Ducart.

It is unique, since its collection of antiques and paintings cannot only be viewed but many can be purchased.

DUNKATHEL is 3½ miles from the city of Cork on the Youghal road.

Italianate splendour in the garden island of Garnish, near Glengarriff

FARRAN FOREST PARK
County Cork

The lovely Farran Forest Park came about because of the huge lake formed by the Inniscarra hydro-electric reservoir scheme in conjunction with the River Lee.

It is an enchanting 130 acres with a former shooting lodge in the centre as a tourist information office. The wildlife enclosures embrace a wide variety of birds and deer.

FARRAN FOREST PARK is 11 miles from the city of Cork.

FOTA ESTATE
County Cork

Fota estate, formerly a private property, was acquired by University College Cork, and today a large portion of it is an imaginative national wildlife park open to the public with a unique bee garden, a splendid arboretum containing some of the finest trees and shrubs in the country, and Fota House itself, with its magnificent collection of Irish period furniture and 18th and 19th-century Irish landscape paintings.

Fota estate was originally the home of the celebrated Smith-Barrys of Cork, and they had their family motto carved in stone at the entrance to the estate, 'Boutez en Avant' — Press on Regardless!

FOTA ESTATE, on Fota island, is 14 miles from Cork city on the road to Cobh.

GLENGARRIFF
County Cork

Glengarriff – the 'Rugged Glen' is one of the most beautiful villages in Ireland, by the sea, and surrounded by majestic mountains. It is in a rocky glen abounding with every variety of mediterranean flower and shrub, including Arbutus and fuchsia in profusion. The glen is heavily wooded with oak, elm, pine, yew and holly. At the entrance to this village on Bantry Bay is the Italianate garden island of Garnish. On this sub-tropical island George Bernard Shaw wrote his play *Saint Joan*. Garnish Island or, as it is sometimes known, *Ilnacullin*, – 'The Island of Holly' – is a 37 acre garden

53

paradise which was, until 1910, a barren rock. Annan Bryce commissioned Harold Peto of Somerset to lay out this dream garden on Italian lines. It took 100 gardeners three years to landscape it with rare shrubs from Australia and New Zealand, as well as magnolias, camellias and rhododendrons, their growth made possible by the warm waters of the Gulf Stream. This subtropical island paradise was given to the nation in 1953.

GLENGARRIFF is 68 miles west of Cork, Garnish Island is 5 minutes offshore by boat.

GOUGANE BARRA
County Cork

Gougane Barra – 'St Finbarr's Hollow' – is a deep, dark lake, surrounded on three sides by the mountain divide of Cork and Kerry, a mile long, and the source of the River Lee. The fourth side of the Lake is a forested valley of immense beauty. It is set amid a forest park of 1000 acres. On the island, in the middle of the lake, was the hermitage of St Finnbarr, patron saint of Cork. This is marked by a small modern oratory joined to the mainland by a causeway. This is a Gaelic speaking area, and at the adjacent Pass of Keimaneigh – *Céim an Fhiadh* – 'the deers' Pass', after the legend that it was leapt by a hunted deer, the men of Ballingeary fought a pitched battle with the Redcoats of Lord Bantry on 11 January 1822.

GOUGANE BARRA is 43 miles west of Cork.

GOUGANE BARRA FOREST PARK
County Cork

Gougane Barra Forest park is on the lake of the same name, and on the mountainous divide between County Cork and County Kerry.

Nature trails are signposted through the magnificent new forests, there are picnic areas and a ring road for motorists from which they can view the entire park.

GOUGANE BARRA FOREST PARK is 2 miles up the valley off the Macroom to Bantry road at the beautifully named Pass of Keimaneigh — 'The Pass of the Deer' — where legend says a fleeing deer leapt from one ridge of the craggy pass to the other to escape the huntsmen.

INISHVICKILLANE ISLAND
County Kerry

Inishvickillane island is famous for its Eagle's Hollow, where the last of the great eagles of Kerry made their home. It is just 40 years since the last magnificent white-tailed sea eagle of Kerry was observed feeding on gulls and fulmars and puffins on the Great Skellig rock.

If Charles Haughey, the distinguished former Taoiseach of Ireland, has his way, at his private residence and estate on Inishvickillane the Kerry Eagles will one day fly again.

He has commissioned a feasibility study to see if this sea eagle could be encouraged to breed on his private island paradise. Hopes are high, since the white-tailed sea eagle was successfully re-introduced on the island of Rhum in Scotland just 11 years ago. These birds were introduced from Norway, and they are said to have been seen on the Blasket islands.

INISHVICKILLANE ISLAND is a privately-owned island (no visitors), but it can be seen from Slea Head on the Dingle peninsular, on the mainland, a helicopter flight away.

KILLARNEY
County Kerry

Killarney is the principal scenic attraction of Ireland. It has three lakes, luxurious woods and vegetation, waterfalls, mountain ranges, valleys, castles, abbeys and a National Park. No cars are allowed inside the National Park and consequently visitors are obliged to view the scenery on foot or from a horse-drawn Killarney jaunting car, which has been described as 'something you hang down out of'. The jarveys who drive them are real Irish characters, the equivalent of the London Cabbie or the New York taxi driver. They are enormously loquacious, knowledgeable, and thirsty!

Killarney town is, in itself, a tourist trap. Its main claim to fame is its Catholic cathedral, designed by Pugin.

Just one and a half miles out on the road to Kenmare is Ross Castle, (14th-century), belonging to Mac-Carthy Mór, who as Lord Muskerry defended it against Cromwellian forces in 1652. It is perfectly situated on a peninsular which extends into the lower lake of Lough Leane. About a mile from the castle is Innisfallen Island, 20 acres of evergreen and holly, a paradise island with the ruins of the 6th-century abbey of St Fallen.

Two and a half miles from the town of Killarney, on the same road to Kenmare, is the entrance to 'Heaven's Reflex', the Killarney National Park of 11,000 acres presented to the nation by its owners Mr and Mrs Bowers Bourne of California, and their Senator son, Arthur Vin-

The beauty of Killarney's three lakes is almost legendary

cent, in 1932. Three miles along the same road are the ruins of Muckross Abbey, founded in 1448 by the chief of Desmond, Donal McCarthy. Muckross House is a superb stately home, now a splendid folk museum on the shores of the Lake, with gorgeous gardens. Five and a half miles along the Kenmare road the waters of the Upper Lake reach the waters of Muckross Lake and Lough Leane in a delightful weir or rapids. Nearby is the Torc waterfall, 60 ft high. In the luxurious parks are herds of native Irish red deer and Japanese sika deer.

Ladies View, 12 miles from Killarney on the Kenmare road, gives a superb view of the Killarney Valley with a vista of the Upper Lake joining the Middle Lake with Lough Leane in the far distance. The other superlative panoramic view of Killarney is from the 400 ft height of Aghadoe Hill, two and a half miles from the town on the Killarney Tralee road. Seven miles from Killarney town, on the Killorglin road is the Gap of Dunloe and Kate Kearney's Cottage, the entrance point to a seven mile trek by pony up this majestic mountain pass amid the Macgillycuddy Reeks, the Tomies and the aptly-named Purple Mountains. The Macgillycuddy – Pronounced 'Mac-le-Cuddy' Reeks include Carrantuohill (3414 ft), Ireland's highest mountain.

KILLARNEY is 191 miles from Dublin via Limerick and Abbeyfeale, 54 miles from Cork and 68 miles from Limerick.

KILLARNEY NATIONAL PARK
County Kerry

Killarney National Park, the most beautiful park in these islands, was originally known as the Bourn Vin-

cent Memorial Park. This priceless gift to the nation of 19,955 acres of woodlands and mountains on the shores of the famous lakes is one of the most generous American gifts to Ireland ever made. Recently more lakes and woodlands have been added to the national collection from the estate of the late Beatrice Grosvenor. Beatrice served in the British Red Cross in World War II and was a distinguished aide to the late Lady Mountbatten.

Because of the proximity of the sea and the mild influence of the waters of the Gulf Stream, Killarney has the most exotic of shrubs in its sheltered places.

Muckross House, once the 'Big House', is at the centre of the main gardens on the shores of Lake Muckross, the second largest of the three main lakes of Killarney. The formal gardens here are rich in rhododendra and azaleas. The park has four signposted nature trails for visitors to walk. They are also permitted to cycle in the park, or to hire a traditional jaunting car (which is a tourist trap!) and motor cars are absolutely forbidden.

The Grosvenor and McShane estates can be approached through Deenagh Lodge opposite Killarney town's magnificent Pugin Cathedral, the main tourist spot in Killarney town.

Muckross House is fortunate in having a cultured and civilised manager with a sense of history, so there are good information offices throughout the area, and a splendid audio visual show in the house itself. *MUCKROSS HOUSE is 3½ miles from Killarney town, on the road to Kenmare.*

Muckross House lies on the shores of Lake Muckross in the heart of Killarney

Charles fort was built in 1677 to protect Kinsale's strategically-important harbour

KINSALE
County Cork

Kinsale is one of the most attractive seaside towns in the county. It is a Georgian town, with a vast harbour always protected by ancient forts such as Charles fort, built in 1677. It was once one of the most important naval bases in these islands. Here, in 1601, the Elizabethan forces of Carew and Mountjoy smashed the Irish forces of the Earls of Tyrone and Tirconnell and their Spanish Allies. The course of the battle can be followed on maps on the bat-

tlefield above Kinsale. In the town is the 12th-century church of St Multose, a Desmond Castle, a 16th-century French prison, and the remains of the Carmelite Friary of 1314. It was off the Old Head of Kinsale, in May 1915, that the liner, the *Lusitania* was torpedoed and sunk by a German submarine.

The founder of the American State of Pennsylvania, William Penn, was clerk of the Admiralty Court of Kinsale, and his father was Governor of Kinsale.

KINSALE is 18 miles south of Cork and 179 miles from Dublin.

MALLOW
County Cork

On the north bank of the River Blackwater, Mallow was made famous by the lilting Irish jig, *The Rakes of Mallow*. It is the hunting centre of the county and has a popular racecourse. Anthony Trollope lived in the town for some time, and among its other celebrated citizens were Thomas Davis, the poet patriot of the Young Ireland movement, Canon Sheehan the novelist, and William O'Brien M.P.

Doneraile, just north of the town,

was a haunt of the poet Spenser, who lived at Kilcolman Castle from 1586 to 1598, where he wrote *The Faerie Queen*. Canon Sheehan, was parish priest of Doneraile from 1895 to 1913.

Buttevant, nearby on the River Awbeg was the 12th-century seat of the Barrys of Cork. Just seven miles away, at Killavullen, on a cliff overlooking the river is the ancestral home of the Hennessy family, the original distillers of the world-renowned brand of cognac.

MALLOW is 22 miles north of Cork and 149 miles from Dublin.

57

PARKNASILLA
County Kerry

Parknasilla – *Pairc an Saileach* – the willow field, is beautifully situated on the north shore of the Kenmare River bay. Renowned for its tropical climate and exotic vegetation, Parknasilla basks in the warm waters of the Gulf Stream. The hotel here was once the home of Charles Graves, protestant bishop of Limerick, father of Alfred Percival Graves, scholar and poet (1846-1931) and grandfather of the poet and novelist Robert Graves. At Sneem, about two miles west on the road to Waterville is the Catholic Church, given by Lord Dunraven, whose parish priest was Father Michael Walsh (1828-1866) the 'Father O'Flynn' of the popular ballad by Alfred Percival Graves. The East window is a memorial to the Limerick born poet Aubrey de Vere (1814-1902), friend of William Wordsworth and Cardinal Newman.
🚗 *PARKNASILLA is about 12 miles west of Kenmare.*

SKELLLIGS ROCKS
County Kerry

Skelligs Rocks – *Na Sceallaga* – the rocks, are three little jagged islands of stone rising out of the Atlantic. Skellig Michael, or Great Skellig, is a massive rocky haunt of puffins, guillemots, petrel and fulmar, 700 ft high, half a mile long, and three quarters of a mile wide. At 540 ft above the landing jetty is the best-preserved and oldest monastic site in Europe. The stone stairs to the site of beehive cells, oratories, cemeteries, holy wells, stone crosses, and the chapel of St Michael are over 1000 years old. The Little Skellig is a bird sanctuary for 20,000 pairs of gannets, the second largest

The Rose of Tralee is a contest for women of typically Irish beauty

gannetry in the North Atlantic. The third island is known as Lemon Rock.
🌿 *THE GREAT SKELLIG is 8 miles west of Bolus head, 12 miles by sea from Portmagee and can be approached by motor boat services from here, and from Reenard, Cahirciveen, or Derrynane.*

TRALEE
County Kerry

Tralee is a thriving town set at the head of the Bay of Tralee and the gateway to the magnificent mountainous peninsular of Dingle. This was the castle home of the Earls of Desmond until it was given over to Sir Edward Denny. The last of the Earls of Desmond finished up with his head on a spike on London Bridge in Elizabethan times.

The town is famous for its International Rose of Tralee Festival, held in September each year. The 'Rose' is in fact a pretty girl, chosen from women of Irish descent all over the world. The festival coincides with the annual four day Tralee horserace meeting. Clogher House, at Ballymullen, near the town, was the home of William Mulchinock (1820-1864), the composer of the world-famous song, *The Rose of Tralee*. In the centre of the town is a garden of roses as a memorial to the composer. The Ashe Theatre, in Denny street, is the leading *Siamsa* or Folk Theatre in Ireland. In St John's Cathedral Church there are magnificent Stations of the Cross by Sean Keating RHA.

About three miles south of the town is the mysterious 'Scotia's Glen'. Historians say that the prehistoric folk of Ireland, the Milesians, landed here in around 3500 B.C. and fought a battle with the mythical Tuatha de Danaan at the foot of the Slieve Mish mountains. The Milesians were victorious but among the dead were Scotia and another princess, Fais. Scotia lies buried in 'Scotia's Glen', and Fais in the mound at Gleann Fhaise, 10 miles south west of Tralee.
🚗 *TRALEE is 20 miles north west of Killarney and 64 miles south west of Limerick.*

WATERVILLE
County Kerry

Waterville – *An Coireán* – the Little Whirlpool, is a charming resort, nestling between the Atlantic Ocean and the 17-mile circumference of Lough Currane. It was a favourite holiday spot of Charlie Chaplin and his family when they lived in Switzerland. On Lough Currane are the ruins of the oratory of the 6th-century St Fintan. Above the lake the mountains rise 2000 ft and more. Waterville is on the famous Ring of Kerry which starts and ends at Killarney, 110 miles of enchanting scenic road encircling the Iveragh Peninsular.
🚗 *WATERVILLE is 39 miles south west of Kenmare and 241 miles from Dublin.*

YOUGHAL
County Cork

The seaside village of Youghal, pronounced 'Yawl', lies at the mouth of the superbly beautiful River Blackwater. Still standing in the town, and in private ownership, is Sir Walter Raleigh's home 'Myrtle Grove', an Elizabethan manor in which he lived while mayor of Youghal, and where he smoked the first tobacco and grew the first potatoes from the New World.
🚗 *YOUGHAL is 30 miles east of Cork.*

Palm trees grow in Parknasilla. This part of the coast enjoys an exotic climate

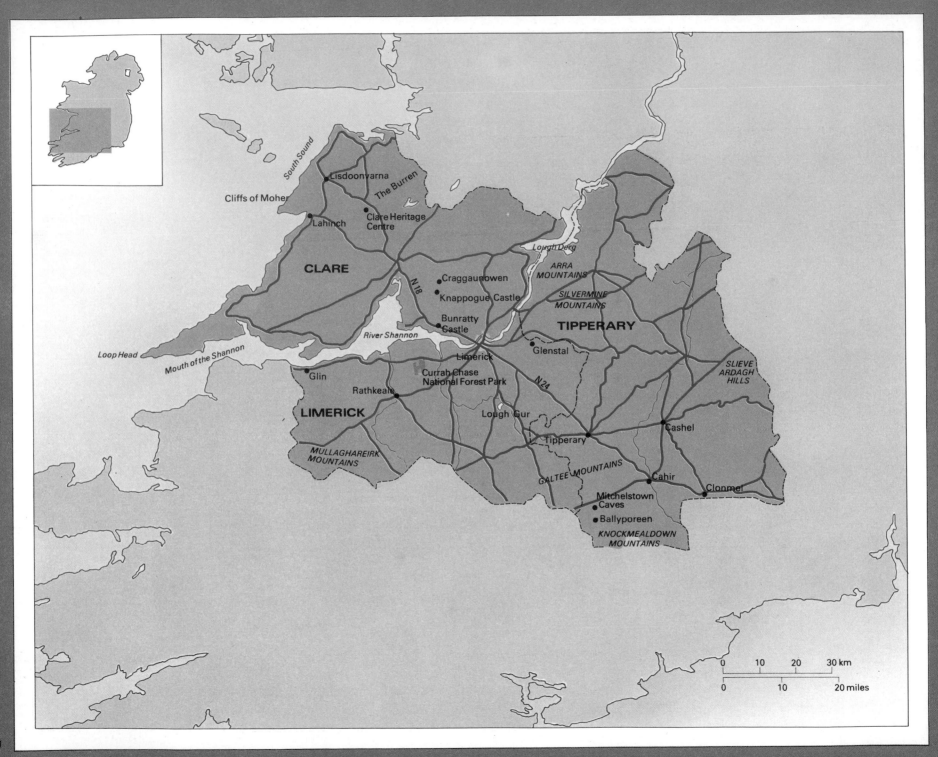

Lisdoonvarna
The Burren
Cliffs of Moher
Clare Heritage Centre
Lahinch
South Sound
CLARE
Lough Derg
ARRA MOUNTAINS
Craggaunowen
N18
Knappogue Castle
SILVERMINE MOUNTAINS
Bunratty Castle
TIPPERARY
River Shannon
Glenstal
Loop Head
Mouth of the Shannon
Limerick
SLIEVE ARDAGH HILLS
Glin
Currah Chase National Forest Park
N24
Rathkeale
LIMERICK
Lough Gur
Cashel
Tipperary
MULLAGHAREIRK MOUNTAINS
GALTEE MOUNTAINS
Cahir
Clonmel
Mitchelstown Caves
Ballyporeen
KNOCKMEALDOWN MOUNTAINS

| 0 | 10 | 20 | 30 km |

| 0 | 10 | | 20 miles |

This beautiful thatched cottage with its neat and tidy frontage has an English look about it, but it is situated in Adare in the heart of County Limerick

THE COUNTY OF CLARE lies on the north bank of the mighty estuary of the Shannon, the longest river in these islands, with its west atlantic coast rising to 700 ft in the Cliffs of Moher, looking out over the Aran islands. It is on the world map because of a little-known spot on the river's estuary called *Rineanna*, now known as Shannon International airport, the first duty-free airport in the world, the modern crossroads between the Old World and the New. Limerick, on the other hand, has achieved fame through three of its citizens, Sean Keating, RHA (1889-1978), the distinguished painter, Kate O'Brien (1897-1974), the novelist, and Lola Montez (1818-1861), the famous dancer, born Marie Gilbert, beloved of the insane King Ludwig I of Bavaria. Its name has passed into the English language as the word for a humorous, often ribald rhyme.

The name 'Tipperary' was appropriated for the nostalgic ballad *It's A Long Way To Tipperary* sung by British troops in the 1914-1918 war. It became popular because of the many Irish regiments who fought in this war with distinction, with a loss of over 50,000 volunteers killed in action. To most Irish people, Tipperary is synonymous with the dairy produce which flows from its 'Golden Vale', for the high profile of its patriotic volunteers in the Anglo-Irish war of Independence, and for being the birthplace of the popular novelist and Fenian, Charles Kickham.

BALLYPOREEN
County Tipperary

Ballyporeen is a charming little village at the foot of the Knockmealdown and Kilworth mountains which is famous for three of its sons. The first is Jack O'Brien, local patriot in the War of Independence, and the founder of what is now the highly acclaimed Irish Tourist Board. The second is Pat O'Brien, the veteran Hollywood film star who always played the 'good guy', the lovable Irish-American Parish Priest, or the likeable US Naval officer. The third is Michael Regan, baptised in the local church in 1829, later to emigrate to England, change his name to Reagan, move to America, and who was the great-grandfather of Ronald Reagan, President of the United States of America. On 3 June 1984, President Reagan visited Ballyporeen and saw for himself, in the Parochial House, the register in which his great grandfather's baptism was recorded on 3 September 1829.

BALLYPOREEN is 8 miles from Mitchelstown and 136 miles from Dublin.

BUNRATTY CASTLE
County Clare

Bunratty Castle is host to twice-nightly elegant and tastefully-presented medieval banquets in which superb traditional musicians and singers appear in period costume. The castle, thanks to its owner, Lord Gort V.C., who purchased it in 1954, and the Irish Tourist Board, has been fully restored to its 16th-century glory, and is furnished with the best selection of period furniture and furnishings in these islands. The whole

Visitors to Bunratty Folk Park can step back in time as they walk along this quaint old street

area around the castle has been transformed into a magnificent folk-park. Here are examples of every kind of Irish thatched cottage, and traditional craftsmen such as black-smiths, candle makers, basket-weavers, and bread makers can be seen at work. This is a living folk park in excellent taste with farm-house teas available.

Originally Bunratty Castle was built on the Ratty river in 1250, by Robert de Muscegros, then held by the de Clare family, and was regularly fought over by the local Irish, the O'Briens and the Macnamaras. The present massive square tower building was erected in

1450 by a Macnamara and taken in 1500 by the O'Brien's, who submitted to Henry VIII. The Shannon Free Airport Development Company Ltd now run the medieval castle enterprise on behalf of the trustees, with any profits from its use by the public going to improvements in the castle. The enormous square building has a huge banqueting hall on the first floor, and another magnificent hall on the second floor with a high 16th-century ceiling, a beautiful chapel (1619) and the living quarters of the great Earl of Bunratty. There are vaulted cellars, and the castle has elegant castellated turrets at its corners.

BUNRATTY CASTLE is 2½ miles from Shannon Airport and 5½ miles west of Limerick city.

CAHIR
County Tipperary

Cahir is a charming market town on the beautiful River Suir, at the foot of the Galtee mountains, with a magnificent 15th-century castle. One of the first to be fully restored in Ireland, it has a massive keep, and is enclosed by high walls with a vast courtyard and hall. It was built in 1142 by Conor O'Brien, Prince of Thomond, and was taken over by the Butlers, Earls of Ormonde. The

Cahir Castle, a splendid 15th-century edifice, seen across the tumbling River Suir

Taking its name from the Irish *Caiseal Muman* — the stone fort of Munster — the Rock of Cashel

castle, which is floodlit at night, is open to the public, and was one of the first restored castles to install explanatory visual aids.

◄ *CAHIR is 14 miles from Tipperary, and 110 miles from Dublin.*

CASHEL
County Tipperary

Cashel is the Irish equivalent to the Acropolis, commonly known as the Rock of Cashel by virtue of its lofty ecclesiastical buildings rising dramatically over the surrounding plain. It was the fortified seat of kings from A.D. 350 to A.D. 1001, when the King of Munster, Murtagh O'Brien, gave the rock to the Church. St Patrick visited it to baptise Aenghus, King of Munster, and gave it a bishop. The most famous Bishop of Cashel was Cormac Mac Cuilleannáin, killed in battle in 908, while attempting to set himself up as High King. Brian Boru was crowned King here in 977. King Cormac McCarthy began the building of Cormac's Chapel in 1127, and it was consecrated in 1134. Domhnall Mór

O'Brien founded a cathedral in 1169, which was replaced by the present cathedral whose framework remains. Gerald Fitzgerald burnt the cathedral down in the late 15th century, because as he explained to King Henry VII, he thought the Archbishop was still inside! The 9th-century Round Tower on the Rock is almost 100 ft high with a circumference of 56 ft. Cormac's chapel is a 12th-century Hiberno-Romanesque gem. St Patrick's Cross, inserted into the coronation stone of Munster Kings, is one of the

most ancient crosses in Ireland. The cathedral is above Cormac's chapel, cross-shaped with a central tower. The Hall of Vicars Choral was built in 1421. St Mary's Abbey, to the west of the Rock, was once a Benedictine monastery established by monks from Glastonbury. St Dominic's Abbey was the first Dominican church to be built in Ireland, in 1243. Cashel Palace, the Deanery, a Queen Anne style building of 1730, was once the residence of the Protestant Archbishops of Cashel, and is now a first class hotel with a reputation for excellent cuisine.

🚗 *CASHEL is 100 miles from Dublin and 12 miles from Tipperary.*

CLARE HERITAGE CENTRE
County Clare

For visitors to the County of Clare looking for their ancestors there is a 'tracing your ancestor' service in the very original interpretive centre in the village of Corofin, in what was once an old Church of Ireland church. Here, living conditions of the ordinary Irish people for the past hundred years and more are explained with audio-visual aids.

They give an insight into rural Ireland, arts and crafts, culture and famine, land tenure and emigration.

🚗 *COROFIN — 'The Weir of Finne' — lies near the shore of Lough Inchiquin, 13 miles from Lahinch and 13 miles from Lisdoonvarna.*

THE CLIFFS OF MOHER
County Clare

The Cliffs of Moher, the most spectacular cliffs in Ireland, stretch for five miles along the rugged Atlantic coast. Formed from massive beds of yellow Moher Shales looking like coal, and reaching a height of 700 ft, they can be easily approached from the landward side by rolling green meadows which suddenly and fearfully drop precipitously into the Atlantic foam. The rich fishing grounds below the vertical cliffs and the slopes and cliff-sides make ideal homes for thousands of nesting guillemot, razorbill, puffin, kittiwake, herring gulls, fulmar, chough, great blackbacked gulls, and even peregrine. The tourist information centre and observation post, O'Brien's Tower, built in 1835 by Cornelius O'Brien, a notorious landlord and MP for Clare, is the ideal spot from which to view the coastline and the Aran islands to the west. On a clear day the view from the tower stretches as far as the Twelve Pins of Connemara to the north, and the mountains of Kerry, due south. The information office is in the capable hands of local, young and knowledgeable people, who also run an excellent souvenir and craft shop. For the very brave there is an excellent 'platform' of flagstones just below the tower from which there is an awesome and precipitous view vertically downwards of the cliffs and their wild-bird inhabitants. On the road from Liscannor to the cliffs is the phallic O'Brien Monument which the eccentric and prolific landlord ordered his tenants to erect in his honour in 1853.

Three miles from the Cliffs of Moher is the tiny fishing village of Liscannor, and on the north shore of Liscannor Bay, the birthplace of John P. Holland (1841-1914), the inventor of the submarine, who emigrated to America.

The beautiful seaside resort of Lahinch lies nearby, home of the south of Ireland championship golf course and the Aberdeen Arms Hotel, famous for its seafood and 'Liscannor Broth.'

🚗 *THE CLIFFS OF MOHER are 3 miles west of Liscannor.*

CLONMEL
County Tipperary

Clonmel, *Cluain Meala* – the 'Honey Meadow', set against the Comeragh Mountains, is one of the most friendly and attractive towns in the county. Guarding the crossing of the River Suir, it has had the usual turbulent history of Norse raids, Anglo-Norman occupation, and

The precipitous Cliffs of Moher

65

assault by Cromwellian forces. In fact, in No. 19 Main Street, once a bishop's palace, the 19th-century owner found in the rafters a number of letters signed by Oliver Cromwell during its occupation in 1650.

Laurence Sterne (1713-1768), author of *A Sentimental Journey* – was born in Clonmel, and George Borrow (1803-1881) went to school in the town. In 1766 the parish priest, Father Nicholas Sheehy, was hanged on trumped up charges by the local landlord, and Lord Lismore called out the military to stop a monument being erected over his grave.

Charles Bianconi, the Italian pedlar turned transport magnate, set up his horse-drawn passenger service from Clonmel, 'Bianconi Cars' and established a nationwide fast transport network.

Clonmel is an important horse and greyhound breeding centre. Horseracing takes place at Powerstown Park Racecourse, and greyhound racing takes place at the track at Davis Road. It is also the hunting centre for the Tipperary Foxhounds and the Clonmel Harriers. It is the centre of the greyhound 'Coursing' world.

The Main Guard, once the town house of the Count Palatine of Tipperary, and in which the main guard was once stationed, was designed by Sir Christopher Wren.

CLONMEL is 105 miles from Dublin and 15 miles from Cashel.

CRAGGAUNOWEN
County Clare

Craggaunowen, little known to the visitor because it is difficult to find, boasts a splendid example of an Irish house of the 15th and 16th centuries; a four-storey tower house which was a fortified Irish home and castle. On

Re-constructed pre-Christian lake dwellings called 'crannogs' can be seen at Craggaunowen

the ground floor is an excellent museum with items from the celebrated Hunt collection of medieval art. Part of the local scheme for the preservation of the past for the visitor is the reconstructed pre-Christian period crannog or lake dwelling. Within the reconstructed ring fort stands an example of the house an ordinary farmer would have lived in 500 years ago, complete with domestic utensils of the period, and an underground passage or souterrain which would have been used as a storage place for food. Irish afternoon teas are available.

The historic complex also houses a leather boat, the sailing ship the *Brendan*, in which Tim Severin followed the route of the 6th-century St Brendan the Navigator's voyage to America.

🚗 *CRAGGAUNOWEN is just off the Quin to Sixmile bridge road, some 15 miles west of Ennis and just north of Knappogue.*

CURRAH CHASE
NATIONAL FOREST PARK
County Limerick

The Forest and Wildlife Service of the Department of Fisheries and Forestry took over the 568 acres of this Forest Park in 1982. The estate has been planted for nearly one hundred years with a wide variety of exotic and unusual trees. The principal trees in this glorious park are sycamore, beech, ash, elm and hornbeam. Within the park is a caravan and camping site and there is a signposted arboretum and nature trails.

This was once the home of the celebrated Irish poet Aubrey de Vere (1814-1902) who was born here, and lived here nearly all his life. Because he was a native of Limerick he was much influenced in his work by his

Glenstal Abbey is a castellated mansion amid grounds of spectacular beauty

quiet life in the magical woods. He was a convert to the religion of the majority of the Irish people, the Roman Catholic faith, and he was to become famous for his English Catholic devotional poetry. In 1897 he published his *Recollections*.

He was much admired, and in the Catholic church of Sneem, in County Kerry, a church built by Lord Dunraven, there is an East window memorial to the poet. Alas, the once splendid and proud 18th-century house of the poet was destroyed by fire in 1941 and only the shell remains. This friend of Tennyson and Wordsworth lies buried in Askeaton in the graveyard of the Protestant

parish church, which was erected on the remains of the Augustinian Pirory of St Mary.

🚗 *CURRAH CHASE PARK is 5 miles from Adare, and 13 miles west of the city of Limerick.*

GLENSTAL
County Limerick

On the hillside north of the village of Murroe – *An Mhá Rua* – the Red Plain, is the Benedictine Abbey of St Columba, with its services open to the public, and a modern centre for the promotion of ecumenism. It is, in its own very quiet way, one of the great civilising influences on the

public and private life of the country through its former students, for it is a school of art and crafts in the liberal tradition.

This magnificent castellated mansion, complete with Black Knight in armour keeping watch from the highest tower of the Windsor Castle-style Norman watch tower and gate, was built in the 19th century by the Barrington family, who founded Barrington's Hospital in Limerick City in 1820. This superb castle, with its surrounding acres of trees and shrubs and artificial lakes was acquired by Benedictine monks from Maredsous, in Belgium in 1926, The hills are alive with colour in 67 rhododendron time, in May and June. The interior includes a library door in stone, a replica of the Hiberno-Romanesque doorway of Killaloe Cathedral. The Abbey church is a riot of colour and contains examples of silver and metal work by the monks.

In the 'Rent an Irish Cottage' scheme in the nearby village of Murroe traditional Irish musical evenings are held during the summer season.

🚗 *GLENSTAL is less than 10 miles east of Limerick City.*

GLIN
County Limerick

Glin is a most attractive village on the southern shores of the Shannon estuary. *An Gleann*, the Glen, takes its name from the Knights of Glin, the Fitzgerald family, whose ancestral home is Glin Castle to the west of the village. They have held land here for over 700 years as the Geraldines of Munster. The present Knight of Glin studied at the Victoria and Albert Museum in London, and is one of the best informed antiquarians in Ireland. The Gothic style lodge of this 1780s castle, on the Tarbert road, is an excellent craft shop and restaurant.

🚗 *GLIN is 8 miles west of Foynes and 31 miles west of Limerick.*

KNAPPOGUE CASTLE
County Clare

Knappogue Castle is one of some 42 castles built by the Clan of McNamara who ruled over Clare from the 5th to the 15th centuries. It was built in 1467 to defend the territory from the advancing Normans. A stout 16th-century tower, it has been fully restored and furnished, and is open to visitors. Twice nightly it is the scene of colourful

Glin Castle, ancestral home of the Fitzgerald family, is set in formal gardens

medieval banquets.

🚗 *KNAPPOGUE is 2¾ miles from Quin, and 8¾ miles east of Ennis.*

LAHINCH
County Clare

Lahinch – *Leacht Ui Chonchubhar* – O'Connor's Cairn, has a magnificent Atlantic sandy beach over one mile in length and perfect for bathing in the huge Atlantic rollers. This is a part of Clare made famous by the novels and stories of Edna O'Brien.

The undulating 18-hole championship golf-links runs all along the spectacular coastline. The barometer in the clubhouse has 'see goats' scrawled on it, as when these gentle tethered animals out on the links seek shelter, it means an Atlantic storm is on its way!

There is a local tradition that a whole village, complete with church and bell-steeple, lies beneath the bay, and you can hear the church bell ringing, very faintly, if you listen hard enough. A lively little resort, it has all amenities such as an entertainment centre, a sea water swimming pool, surfing facilities and a theatre.

Just five miles south, along the coast, is *Rinn na Spainneach*, Spanish Point, named for six huge ships of the Spanish Armada which were wrecked on the rocks in 1588. A thousand sailors perished, and their graves are marked by mounds and boulders in the fields beside the sea. Those who did not perish by drowning were put to the sword on the orders of the Elizabethan Governor of Connacht, Sir Turlough O'Brien, Boetius Clancy, Sheriff of Clare and their men.

🚗 *LAHINCH is 19 miles west of Ennis on a narrow road.*

The Burren

The Burren – *Boireann* – the Great Rock, is the name given to a 200 square mile lunar landscape of grey limestone forming one of the most unusual natural rock gardens in the world. It is bordered by Galway Bay in the north, the Atlantic Ocean, and its extension, the Aran Islands in the west, and Gort, in County Galway in the north east. The old saying is that in the Burren there is not a tree on which to hang a man, water enough in which to drown him, or earth enough in which to bury him. In the cracks and fissures of the rocks, protected from wind and frost, grow a profusion of exotic wild flowers. They include Mountain Avens, Spring Gentian, Mossy Saxifrages, Maidenhair, Close-flowered Orchids, Bloody Crane's-bill, Hart's tongue, Madder, Hoary Rock-rose, and Pyramidal Bugle, and rare moths and butterflies thrive here. This land of Alpine and other types of rare flowers is not only of interest to the botanist but also to the geologist, speleologist, archaeologist and entomologist. May and June are the months in which to see this natural flower show at its best.

There are over 700 dolmens and stone forts on this lunar landscape and massive underground caves, notably the two million BC Aillwee cave (open to the public). At Kilfenora, a village in the heart of the Burren country, is a Display Centre open to the public for the study and interpretation of this unique natural rock garden.

The Burren — a strange moonscape of grey limestone

Many exotic wild flowers grow in the warm climate of the Burren

St John's Castle on the banks of the River Shannon in Limerick

LIMERICK
County Limerick

Limerick City began in the 9th century as a Norse settlement on the River Shannon which was recaptured for the Irish by King Brian Boru. It then became an Anglo-Norman stronghold in 1175, commanding the vital bridge across the River Shannon. The greatest and most tragic years in its history were during the Jacobite-William of Orange wars from 1689 to 1691. In 1691 the Irish garrison surrendered to the Williamite forces of the Dutch general Ginkel, after the signing of the Treaty of Limerick. The garrison of 11,000 marched out with full battle honours to join the armies of King Louis of France, the beginning of an era which was to see half a million Irish soldiers join 'The Wild Geese', to serve in foreign armies.

Modern Limerick has effected many remarkable changes. In Michael Street, for example, an 18th-century Georgian granary has been tastefully transformed to modern usage and houses the Tourist Information Office and shopping, dining and entertainment facilities. Across Matthew Bridge, near the granary, is the Cathedral of St Mary, founded in 1176 by Donal Mor O'Brien, King of Munster, who granted his palace for its building. The carved choir stalls are 15th century. There are numerous 15th-century tombs including that of Murrough O'Brien, the infamous 'O'Brien of the Burnings' who laid waste the Province of Munster as the Earl of Inchiquin (1618-1674). A *Son et Lumiere* presentation tells the story of the cathedral. St John's Castle, in Castle Street, was built by the Normans in 1200. Five sided, it has one complete side on the waters of the Shannon and was established to guard the Thomond Bridge. On the other side of Thomond Bridge, from St John's Castle, on the west side, is a roughly-hewn stone mounted on a pedestal which is said to be the stone on which the surrender treaty of 1691 was signed. On the west side of St John's Square numbers 1 and 2 contain the Limerick Museum with its impressive collection of historical

These mock neolithic dwellings on Lough Gur's shores house an imaginative interpretive centre

material. At the Good Shepherd Convent in Clare Street, on the Dublin road, superb examples of Limerick lace can be seen. The 18th-century craft lives on in Limerick. In the National Institute for Higher Education, not far from the city centre, off the Dublin road, is the modern Hunt Museum housing 1000 items from the collection donated by John Hunt, the art historian and Celtic/Norman archaeologist.

The 'temporary' wooden church on the Ennis road is little known and yet incorporates some magnificent examples of modern Irish ecclesiastical art. These include the teak statue of 'Our Lady of Fatima' by Oisín Kelly, the 'Annunciation' by Imogen Stuart, the 'Deposition' by Andrew O'Connor, the 'Sacred Heart' and 'Our Lady' by Yvonne Jammet, and the baptistry window, the 'Baptism of Christ' by Evie Hone.

The Belltable Arts Centre in O'Connell Street is a venue for theatre and for exhibitions, and at *An Chistin*, in Thomas Street, there is superb traditional Irish music.

LIMERICK *is 123 miles south west of Dublin, and 65 miles north of Cork.*

LISDOONVARNA
County Clare

Lisdoonvarna – *Lios Duin Bhearna* – the Enclosure of the Gap-Fort, is an amazing spa possessing unique health-giving waters. Its spring waters include sulphur, magnesia and iron, and all the waters contain iodine. The Spa Wells Health Centre has a pump house and baths, and there is a special pump room for the magnesia spring. There are sauna baths, showers, sun lounges, beauty therapy and massage centres, and it is noted for the number of jockeys who undergo fitness courses here.

In the autumn the town is inundated with Irish farmers seeking a wife, after the harvest is in. There is an annual festival of Irish bachelors who dance jigs and swill Guinness all night in the company of the visiting and local women who are hoping to find Mr Right.

LISDOONVARNA *is 23 miles from Ennis 167 miles from Dublin via Limerick and Ennis.*

LOUGH GUR
County Limerick

Lough Gur is a tiny U-shaped lake on whose shores archaeologists have discovered how people lived some 2-300 years BC and, in modern times, an excellent interpretive centre, designed like neolithic houses, has been built to provide visual aids with commentaries and music. The 'neolithic' thatched houses, one circular and one rectangular, include a tourist information office, and there is an admission charge. There are some 30 monuments around the lake in the form of stone circles, forts, dolmens, megalithic tombs, standing stones and pre-historic dwellings. The principal attraction is the stone circle in the town land of Grange. In diameter it is one of the larger stone circles in Ireland designed for some now-forgotten ritual. It dates from 2000 BC, and pottery of this age has been found inside the circle.

Tempall Nua, the New Church, is 15th century, and has been repaired. The 17th-century harpist, Tomas O Connalláin who composed *Limerick's Lament*, is buried in this churchyard. *Carraig Aille* is a stone

71

fort in an irregular circle, dating from the 8th or 9th centuries. A hoard of Norse silver was discovered on the site, and evidence of iron smelting. The Giants Cave is a wedge-shaped gallery grave divided into two chambers. Near the entrance to the lake stands the 15th-century Bouchier's Geraldine castle. Bolin Island is, in fact, an artificial island as it is a crannog or lake dwelling constructed by man. In the middle of the U-shaped lake is Garret Island, named after Garret Fitzgerald, not the present Irish Taoiseach, but Geroíd, 4th Earl of Desmond. In the Red Cellar Cave the bones of brown bear and other extinct animals such as giant Irish deer and reindeer have been found.

There are many stone age habitations and burial mounds, some of which have yielded up burial urns dating from 1500 BC. 'The Spectacles' are the foundations of the formation of Early Christian huts.

🚗 *LOUGH GUR is 12 miles south of Limerick City.*

MITCHELSTOWN CAVES
County Tipperary

Re-discovered in 1833, these massive caves are a monument to what water can do underground over the centuries to a limestock rock area. They are made up of three gigantic caverns, one is 200 ft by 160 ft and 60 ft high, and feature stalactites, stalagmites, huge columns, one called 'The Tower of Babel'.

The 'Desmond' Cave is the one in which the 'Sugán Earl' of Desmond took refuge in 1601 with a huge price on his hunted head. Arthur Young, the celebrated English traveller, visited the caves in 1777 and Martel, the French speleologist made a sketch plan of them.

🚗 *THE CAVES are 3½ miles from*

Ballyporeen in County Tipperary, and about 9 miles from Mitchelstown in County Cork.

RATHKEALE
County Limerick

Rathkeale is a pleasant market town on the River Deel in rich agricultural land. The Earls of Desmond, the Fitzgeralds, owned these lands and their castles, and Sir Walter Raleigh, then Captain Raleigh, commanded the English forces here, who were marched out to massacre the Spanish at Smerwick Harbour in County Kerry in 1580. Castle Matrix, just south-west of Rathkeale, is a Geraldine Castle, built in 1410, and deserves to be more widely known. It has been fully restored by its owner, a military historian, and the splendid library contains the finest collection in existence of documents and weapons relating to the 'Wild Geese', the exiled Irish swordsmen who served with distinction in the Continental armies of the 17th and 18th centuries. It was here that the poet Spenser first met Sir Walter Raleigh, and it is probable that in the rich soil of the Castle grounds the first potato was grown in Ireland.

At the village of Ardagh, just four miles south of Castle Matrix, in an ancient ring fort, the famous 8th-century Ardagh Chalice, brooches and a bronze cup were found.

🚗 *RATHKEALE is 18 miles south west of Limerick.*

TIPPERARY
County Tipperary

Tipperary – *Tiobraid Arann* – The Well of Ara, lays no claim to accidental fame by its inclusion in a popular 1914-1918 British Army marching song, but rests its case for

The fast, exciting game of hurling is Ireland's national sport...

Here Tipperary take on Cork

recognition on both being at the very heart of the fertile Golden Vale dairy lands of the county on the River Ara, and as the gathering place of patriots, novelists and writers. It is a straggling town of the people. King John built a castle here, it was laid waste in Elizabethan wars, survived the Land League Agrarian war, when the tenants of local landlord Smith-Barry tried to build a 'New Tipperary' outside the town, and produced military leaders for the New Ireland. Charles James Kickham (1826-1882) has the place of honour in the town, a bronze, seated figure on a limestone base, with the inscription, 'Charles Kickham, poet, novelist, and, above all, patriot,' erected in 1898. Kickham wrote the most popular of all Irish novels *Knocknagow*, into which he put all his love of the country. James O'Neill, father of the Irish-American dramatist Eugene O'Neill, was born on a farm adjacent to the town. John O'Leary, (1830-1907) Fenian patriot and journalist extraordinary, who converted Yeats to Irish nationalism, was a native of the town. Tipperary was also the headquarters of *Muintir na Tire* (the people of the land) founded in 1931 by Canon John Hayes (1888-1957) who was parish priest of the adjacent village of Bansha. Hurling and Gaelic Football are played in the town's Sean Tracy Park. Limerick Junction Racecourse is just two miles away, and the internationally-famous Scarteen Black and Tan Foxhounds hunt across this district.

Tipperary town is beautifully situated at the north of the wooded Slievenamuck Hills, which rise to 1216 ft, and just north of the superb Glen of Aherlow.

TIPPERARY is 112 miles from Dubin and 25 miles from Limerick.

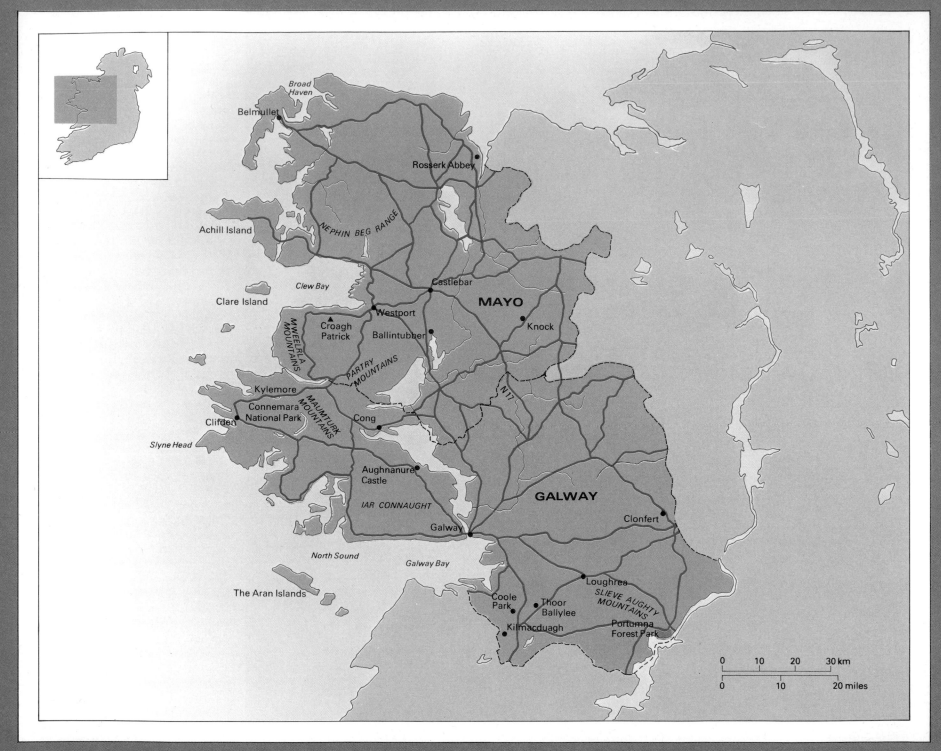

Broad
Haven

Belmullet

Rosserk Abbey

Achill Island

NEPHIN BEG RANGE

Clew Bay

Castlebar

MAYO

Clare Island

Westport

Croagh
Patrick

*MWEELRLA
MOUNTAINS*

Ballintubber

Knock

*PARTRY
MOUNTAINS*

Kylemore

*MAUMTURK
MOUNTAINS*

N17

Connemara
National Park

Cong

Clifden

Slyne Head

Aughnanure
Castle

IAR CONNAUGHT

GALWAY

Clonfert

Galway

North Sound

Galway Bay

Loughrea

The Aran Islands

*SLIEVE AUGHTY
MOUNTAINS*

Coole
Park

Thoor
Ballylee

Kilmacduagh

Portumna
Forest Park

| 0 | 10 | 20 | 30 km |

| 0 | 10 | 20 miles |

The West of Ireland

The tranquil waters of picturesque Lough Corrib, in County Galway, its surface still as a pond

TRADITION HOLDS THAT in Galway City, at the Collegiate Church of St Nicholas, set up by the Anglo Normans in 1320 and enlarged in the 16th century, Christopher Columbus heard mass, and took with him a Galway man, Rice de Culvy, as his navigator to assist him in his voyage of discovery to the New World. Many of the houses of Galway city today retain their Spanish appearance, reflecting the centuries-old trading links between Galway and Spain. Behind the city lies the wild hinterland of Connacht, largely Irish-speaking. The Atlantic rollers pound the indented coastline. The 12 blue Bens, or Pins, of Connemara dominate the lakelands and the skyline. Here the traditions and customs of old Ireland are preserved in a scenic wonderland which includes the most western tip of Celtic Europe, the Aran islands.

Mayo, adjacent, and to the north, is majestic fjord coast with massive bays from Killary to Killala, in which many giant ships of the Spanish Armada foundered in violent storms. Mayo is dominated by Croagh Patrick, St Patrick's holy mountain, rising to a spectacular cone, over 2500 ft high, still easily climbable today. Thousands of pilgrims ascend it annually, striving to reach its sparkling quartzite peak. From the summit is a God's eye view of the west coast of Ireland from the mountains of Kerry in the deep south, to the mountains of Donegal in the far north.

Achill Island is crowned by heather-topped mountains

ACHILL ISLAND
County Mayo

Achill Island, the largest of Irish islands, at over 36,000 acres, 15 miles long and 12 miles wide, is an isle of magnificently wild Atlantic beauty. Crowned by a heather covered mountain range over 2000 ft high, including Slievemore (2204 ft), Croaghaun (2192 ft), Minaun (1530 ft) and gigantic cliffs 800 ft high, the island is joined to the mainland by the slim Michael Davitt Bridge. An ideal centre for hang-gliding and deep sea angling there are beautiful beaches, lake-ringed settlements, cloud-capped mountains, and sun drenched villages. Achill Sound has four excellent trout lakes. Dugort is a magnificent strand, above which towers Slievemore mountain. The area abounds in pre-Christian tombs and cairns. Keem Bay is the haunt of basking sharks. Dooagh bay is famous for its salmon netting.

Corrymore House, near Dooagh, on the slopes of Croaghaun mountain, was once the home of Captain Boycott, who was shunned by the people during the Land League days of the 1880s, and thus gave a new word to the English language.

Keel village has a three mile sandy strand, and the 800 ft high Minaun Cliffs, at low tide, provide a breathtaking view of the Cathedral Rocks. This is the island of Atlantic fishermen, with their haunting ballad sessions.

ACHILL ISLAND is 17 miles west of Newport.

THE ARAN ISLANDS
County Galway

The three islands of Aran lie in Galway Bay; Inishmore, (7635 acres), Inishmaan (2252 acres) and Inisheer (1400 acres). They are Irish-speaking islands made famous by J.M. Synge (1871-1909) in his classic play *Riders to the Sea*, set on Inishmaan, and by Robert Flaherty who made his film *Man of Aran* in 1934. Liam O'Flaherty, the short story writer and author of *The Informer*, was born on Inishmore in 1896. The fishermen of the islands are famous for their frail lath and tarred canvas boats known as 'currachs', their homespun oiled wool 'bawneen' coats, shoes of rough hide, 'pampooties', and colourful woollen belts, the 'crios'. Kilronan, on Inishmore, is capital of the islands. Inishmore has the most westerly prehistoric fort in Europe, Dun Aengus, semi-circular, with its back to the sheer 300 ft cliff drop into the Atlantic Ocean. The fort was composed of ring after ring of stone defence walls, of which the inner court wall remains, 150 ft in diameter with a wall 20 ft high and 18 ft thick. The islands abound in pre-Christian stone forts, early Christian hermitages and tiny monastic churches.

THE ARAN ISLANDS are 30 miles from Galway and can be reached by steamer service from Galway city, motor-boat from Rossaveal, or by frequent twin-engined Aer Arann planes from Galway's Carnmore airport.

AUGHNANURE CASTLE
County Galway

On the western shore of Lough Corrib, on the River Drimneen, stands the beautifully-preserved castle of Aughnanure. Originally it was erected as a stark, stone, square fortress some four storeys high by the 'ferocious O'Flahertys' in the 16th century. It has stout inner and outer

The ruins of St Enda's Church on Inishmore in the Aran Islands

Castlebar's tree-lined Mall is a pleasant place to while away a summer's afternoon

walls and the O'Flaherty's took good care of the inner man with an enormous banqueting hall, most of which remains, but some of which vanished into the River Drimneen.

🚗 *THE CASTLE stands 2 miles south east of Oughterard.*

BALLINTUBBER
County Mayo

Ballintubber – *'Baile Tobair Phádraig'* – the townland of the well of Patrick, as its name implies, is the name of a well spring in which St Patrick baptised the pagan Mayo men and women in 441 and where

he built a church. It was closely associated with Croagh Patrick, and there was at one time a pilgrim road known as Tóchar Phádraig, 20 miles long, to the 'Reek'. Ballintubber Abbey is known as 'The Abbey that refused to die', as mass has been celebrated there for over 760 years without a break. The Abbey is cruciform in shape with transepts, nave and choir. The main doorway is Early Gothic with a high gable, and there are eight early pointed windows. The windows above the altar are Norman, and at the end of the south transept are monastic buildings. The Abbey was founded

in 1216 by the King of Connacht, Cathal More of the wine red hand, for the Canons Regular of St Augustine. The Viscounts Mayo are buried here, and there is a tomb to the son of Grace O'Malley the Pirate Queen, *Tiobód na Long*, Theobald of the Ships. He was a Bourke, son of her second husband, and died in 1629, having been made Viscount Mayo in 1627. Despite being burnt twice, supressed in 1542, and unroofed in Penal times, the Abbey was never abandoned by priest and people.

Just two miles to the south east are the remains of Castle Bourke,

fortress of Myles Bourke, the 4th Viscount Mayo. Nine miles south are the remains of Moore Hall, on the east shore of Lough Carra, birthplace of the novelist George Moore. His remains are buried in a cairn of solid rock on Castle island, at the north end of Lough Carra. One of his ancestors was John Moore (1763-1799), who was President of the Republic of Connacht, set up in Castlebar, when the forces of Napoleon landed at Killala in 1798.

🚗 *BALLINTUBBER is 9½ miles north of Ballinrove, 1 mile off the Ballinrobe to Westport road.*

BELMULLET
County Galway

Belmullet, shaped like a sea-urchin, with Broad Haven Bay at its head and Blacksod Bay at its tail, is a neck of land embracing magnificent sandy beaches, wild headlands and cliff-top forts. It is as serenely wild and beautiful today as the day in September 1588, when one of the Spanish Armada's proudest ships, *La Rata Santa Maria Encoronada*, 820 tons, with 35 guns, ran aground in Blacksod Bay and was fired by her Captain, Don Alonso de Leira.

BELMULLET is 39 miles west of Ballina.

CASTLEBAR
County Mayo

Castlebar – *Caislean an barraig* – Barry's Castle, is the capital of Mayo county, with a pleasant tree-lined Mall. It was founded by the de Barra family, then taken over by John Bingham, the ancestor of the Earls of Lucan in the 17th century. The present-day holder of the title is an infamous Missing Person. The Green in the centre of the town was once a cricket pitch when the Lord Lucans were in residence. It achieved fame curing the 1798 Rebellion when the joint Irish-French forces took over the area and the French troops landed in Killala. The Humbert Inn is named after the French General who won the battle known as the 'Races of Castlebar', as, initially the Redcoats ran. John Moore, the 'President' of the short-lived Republic of Connacht is buried in the Mall. The Linen Hall, now the Town Hall, recalls the days when the town was the centre of the linen industry. The Education Centre was once a chapel whose foundation stone was laid by John Wesley.

The lush greenery of Clare Island is broken only by tiny whitewashed cottages

Michael Davitt founded the Land League in the town in 1879. A commemorative plaque in the Mall marks the house in which Margaret Burke Sheridan (1889-1958), the Prima Donna of La Scala, Milan, and the greatest interpreter of the role of Madame Butterfly, was born.

Louis Brennan, (1852-1932), the inventor of the torpedo, and of the gyroscopic monorail, was born in Main Street, Castlebar. Ernie O'Malley, (1898-1957) revolutionary and author, was born in the town. He is best remembered for his saga, *On Another Man's Wound.*

CASTLEBAR is 11 miles north west of Westpoint and 12 miles from Newport.

CLARE ISLAND
County Mayo

Clare Island, roughly 4000 acres in area, lies at the south of the many-islanded Clew Bay, an isle of tranquillity connected to the mainland by a daily boat service from Roonagh Point, near Louisberg. The island was the headquarters of the Elizabethan Pirate Queen, Grace O'Malley (1530-1600). When her father, Owen O'Malley, chieftain of the barony of Murrisk died, she took over power, and at the age of 16 married Donal O'Flaherty of Bunowen Castle. She attacked rich merchant ships on their way to Galway, and traded with Spain and Portugal. She later married the chief of the Mayo Burkes, Sir Richard Burke and took over his Rockfleet castle. She visited Queen Elizabeth at Hampton Court in 1593 and declined to be made a countess on the grounds that she was already an Irish Queen!

Her O'Malley three storey castle still stands above the harbour on the east coast of the island. She died in 1600 and lies buried in the Carmelite

Clare Abbey, one and a half miles south west of the harbour. The south coast of the island is extremely beautiful, with a range of precipitous cliffs. Knock Mountain drops 1550 ft into the sea. Her fortress home on the mainland, at Carraigahowley Castle, near Newport, was restored by Sir Owen O'Malley in recent years, and is now a national monument.

CLARE ISLAND is roughly 4 miles by sea from Roonagh Quay on the mainland.

CLIFDEN
County Galway

Accepted as the 'capital' of Connemara, Clifden is an attractive village made famous by Ethel Mannin in her novel *Late Have I Loved Thee*, which she wrote in her cottage on Mannin Bay. Perched on the white strands of the Atlantic and set against a backdrop of mountains of incomparable beauty, Thackeray described it as 'one of the most beautiful districts that it is ever the fortune of a traveller to examine'. It is the centre for the annual Connemara Pony Show, held in August. A few miles south of the town, at Derrygimlagh Bog, there is a stone cairn in the shape of the tail of an aeroplane which marks the spot where those intrepid airmen, Alcock and Brown landed their old World War I converted Vickers bomber, to conclude the first non-stop trans-Atlantic flight in June 1919.

CLIFDEN is 49 miles north west of Galway.

CLONFERT
County Galway

Clonfert, almost on the banks of the Shannon river, has the remains of a renowned monastic settlement

80 **Thackeray praised the incomparable beauty of Clifden and its environs**

Ashford Castle, an 18th-century castellated mansion, is now a superb hotel

established in 558 by St Brendan the Navigator. The remains of the 11th-century cathedral are incorporated in the present Church of Ireland building. The chief glory is the west doorway, superbly Hiberno-Romanesque, incorporating a high triangular pediment above the eight pillars and rounded recesses of the semi-circular doorway. In this triangular area are a series, one above the other, of five layers of

carved heads peaking finally in a single carved head. This has direct symbolic links with the old Celtic pagan custom of the cult of the severed human head. By this the severed heads of enemies were placed on carved niches of pagan temples, in the belief that to possess the skull of an enemy meant the possession of power, since the head was deemed the dwelling place of the soul.

CLONFERT is 1 mile north of Ballinasloe, 43 miles of Galway.

CONG
County Mayo

Cong – *Cunga* – a neck, gets its name from being on the isthmus between the Lakes of Mask and Corrib which are the finest free trout fishing waters in Europe. Cong achieved international fame in 1951 when the

Irish-American film director, John Ford, filmed *The Quiet Man* in the area, featuring Maureen O'Hara, John Wayne and Barry Fitzgerald. Cong Abbey was founded in the 12th century by the King of Connacht, Turlough Moore O'Connor. It was rebuilt by another King of Connacht, and in 1203 Rory O'Connor, the last High King of Ireland, died there in retirement. An east window and four doorways are all

81

that remain of the Augustinian monastery which was built on the site of the 7th-century monastic settlement of St Feichin. In the tiny village is the medieval Market Cross erected in the 14th century. The modern Catholic church adjacent to the Abbey has superb Irish stained glass windows by Harry Clarke. The priceless processional Cross of Cong, now in the National Museum in Dublin, was made in Roscommon in 1123 for the Cathedral of Tuam, on the orders of King Turlough O'Connor, to enshrine a relic of the True Cross sent to him from Rome.

His son, Roderick, brought it to Cong, a reliquary of great beauty of oak and copper and decorated with Celtic designs in gold filigree work.

Ashford Castle, recently voted the best hotel in Europe, an 18th-century castellated mansion, was built by the Browne family, and then purchased from the Lord Oranmore and Browne by Sir Benjamin Guinness, who in 1905 entertained the Prince of Wales, later to become King George V. The hotel reached its greatest days of *haute cuisine* and service when it was first run as a hotel by Noel Huggard and his wife. It was then bought by the Irish American millionaire John A Mulcahy, who entertained his friend President Nixon of the United States there on his Irish-American vote-catching visit to the 'Auld Sod'. It is now owned by Tony 'Heinz' O'Reilly and his fellow directors. The lakeside setting is perfection, the interior is elegant and the grounds are beautiful. Cong is also famous for its unique Dry Canal, four miles long. It was built in the 1840s as famine relief work.

The Irish Viceroy himself performed the opening ceremony, and when the lock gates opened, the waters which were to link Loughs Mask and Corrib disappeared through the porous limestone bed!

President Reagan and his wife Nancy spent a relaxing evening in Ashford Castle on their visit to Ireland on 1 June 1984.

There are some 40 underground caves to be explored in Cong.

CONG is 28 miles north of Galway.

CONNEMARA
County Galway

Connemara is the name given to what is generally accepted as the most beautiful part of Galway, the western area between the vast Lake Corrib and the Atlantic ocean. It is dominated by the blue ridge mountains of the 'Twelve Pins' or 'Twelve Bens' of Connemara, which have been captured on canvas in the oil paintings of Paul Henry (1876-1958) the celebrated Irish landscape painter. Largely Irish-speaking, the local people are renowned for their skill at May fly fishing for trout on Lough Corrib, which is also famous for salmon angling. The touring road of Connemara is roughly a figure eight over an area of 30 square miles to the north west of Galway city. It runs west along the Corrib to Oughterard, through Maam Cross, Recess and Ballynahinch to Clifden, returning through Letterfrack and Kylemore to Galway. Ballynahinch Castle was once the home of the Martin family whose most famous member was 'Humanity Dick' Martin, the founder of the Royal Society for the Prevention of Cruelty to Animals.

CONNEMARA lies to the north west of Galway city.

The Blue Ridge Mountains of Connemara are known as The Twelve Bens or Pins

Knock Shrine

Knock –*Cnoc Mhuire* – Mary's Hill, in the middle of the plain of Mayo, 37 miles north of Galway city, is the Irish 'Lourdes', attracting 750,000 visitors every year. This is where Pope John Paul II made his historic visit to Ireland in 1979, visiting the shrine by helicopter on 30 September.

The story of Knock began at 7pm on the evening of Thursday 21 August 1879, when a girl called Mary Beirne, and her companion, Mary McLoughlin, were walking past the gable end of the old parish church, and on the wall, in a globe of light,

they saw the figures of the Virgin Mary, St Joseph and St John the Evangelist, the latter bearing in his arms a lamb. They gathered 15 friends to see these silent figures, which appeared dry in the midst of the driving rain. Mgr. James Horan, the parish priest of the vast modern basilica which stands in the prosperous village today, sees in this alleged vision a parallel with contemporary Ireland, as the Virgin Mary appeared at a time of violence. To the hundreds of thousands of present-day visitors to the village of Knock the main attraction is

to see the 'Wall of Apparitions', now portrayed by figures in stone on the glass-enclosed gable end of the old parish church. The huge new basilica of 'Our Lady, Queen of Ireland', has an encircling ambulatory supported by 40 pillars of stone from every county in Ireland, and has accommodation for 20,000 people. The Basilica is set amid a landscaped parkland where impressive candlelight processions are held in honour of 'Our Lady of Silence', so named because she said nothing when she appeared. She gave no message.

Worshippers at the Shrine of Our Lady in the village of Knock

CONNEMARA NATIONAL PARK
County Galway

Unknown to many visitors, Connemara National Park covers 5000 acres of land south of the Leenane to Clifden main road. There are superb nature trails, signposted long walks and signposted short walks, all amid glorious scenery embracing sea, mountain and lake. A helpful and informative visitor centre is located at Letterfrack, in a splendidly-converted farmhouse and outhouses. These converted farm buildings have flagged floors of Liscannor slate and traditional Irish style furnishings, including the famous 'sugán' chairs. There are audio visual presentations about the area.

LETTERFRACK is 9 miles north east of Clifden on the T71.

COOLE PARK
County Galway

Although Coole Park, the former home of Lady Augusta Gregory (1859-1932) no longer exists, as it was vandalised during World War II, the outline of where the house once stood remains and the long avenue of overhanging yew trees leading up to it. On one of the copper beeches are the initials, beautifully preserved, of some of Lady Gregory's famous guests and visitors, such as George Bernard Shaw, John Masefield, Sean O'Casey, Douglas Hyde, Oliver St John Gogarty, Augustus John, W.B. Yeats, J.M. Synge, Violet Martin and Katharine Tynan. Next to Coole House, in the National Forest and Wildlife Park, is the beloved lake of W.B. Yeats whose poem on the swans of Coole immortalised it, and swans are still there today.

There is, in the fields beside this

Croagh Patrick is Ireland's Holy Mountain. St Patrick fasted on its summit for 40 days and 40 nights

lake an almost physical presence of the greatest revival in Irish literature ever begun, and in which the little Old Lady of Coole Park played such a huge part. Near Coole is the national school house at Kiltartan, and its 15th-century church. Listening to the accents of the children of Galway attending this school gave Lady Gregory the idea of a uniform Irish dialect for the actors in her plays. This has been described as 'Kiltartanese'.

COOLE PARK is about 2 miles from the village of Ardrahan, on the Galway to Limerick road, 18 miles south of Galway and 8 miles north of Gort.

CROAGH PATRICK
County Mayo

Croagh Patrick, (2510 ft) Ireland's Holy Mountain, stands out sharply, the white path to the summit clearly visible all the way from the shores

of Clew Bay. St Patrick fasted on the small summit of this mighty mountain for 40 days and 40 nights, and every year, on the last Sunday of July, thousands of pilgrims, many in their bare feet, climb the holy mountain to hear mass in the passing clouds. There is a chapel on the summit. The view from the top is most rewarding with the many-islanded Clew Bay at the foot, Clare Island, Achill Island, and, on a clear day as far as the blue mountains of

Donegal in the north, and the towering ranges of the Kerry mountains in the deep south. The pilgrim path is a fairly arduous and steady climb, and only very near the summit, where the quartzite shale is broken up into sharp pieces, is the steady walk reduced to a scramble on all fours!

The locals refer to the mountain as 'The Reek' The legend is that it was from this mountain St Patrick banished all the snakes in Ireland, and, after successfully wrestling with the Devil, was promised by the Good Lord that he would be allowed to sit with him on Judgement Day to judge the Irish people, who would never lose the Christian faith.

🚗 CROAGH PATRICK *is 6 miles west of Westport.*

GALWAY
County Galway

Galway gets its name from the River Corrib, on which it stands. Ptolemy put it on his world map as 'Magnata', and the local O'Halloran clan included it in their territories until the Anglo-Norman, Richard de Burgh, took it in 1232. It was a walled city, and the prevailing winds made it easy for an enormous sea trade to grow up between Spain and Galway, so much so that Spanish traders had homes in Galway and Irish traders had them in Spain, and there was much inter-marriage between the two countries. Richard II granted the city a charter in 1484. The Anglo-Norman families who rán the city were known as the 'Tribes of Galway', and they included the Blakes, Bodkins, Brownes, D'Arcy's, ffrenches, Kirwans, Joyces, Lynches, Morrisses, Martins, and Skerrets. These settlers kept themsleves pure from the native Irish, and a bye-law of 1518 declared that 'neither O nor Mac shall strutte ne swagger thro the streets of Galway'.

The native Irish made regular raids, so much so that over the West Gate of the city an inscription read 'From the fury of the O'Flahertys, good Lord deliver us'. Such was the inter-trade over the centuries with Spain, particularly in the smuggling of wines and brandies, silks, laces and tobacco, that there is a strong Iberian influence on the people, the architecture and the manners of to-

Hundreds of salmon can be seen leaping to the spawning grounds upstream at Galway salmon weir

day's Galwegians. So many young Irishmen were smuggled to the Continent and returned as expert swordsmen that in Williamite times the rules of duelling by pistol were drawn up. This was necessary because the young Catholic expert swordsmen, trained in Europe and returned home to Ireland, were challenging their Protestant Ascendancy landowning heirs and decimating them in sword play, so that the 'back-to-back' and shots at twenty paces was agreed as a new form of duelling to make things more equal in affairs of honour.

There is much to be seen in this Spanish-style city. The Collegiate Church of St Nicholas in Lombard Street, erected by the Anglo-Normans in 1320, is remarkable for its unique triple nave. The modern Cathedral of St Nicholas and Our Lady of the Assumption, built on the site of the old city jail, beside the famous salmon weir, is of cut limestone with Connemara marble flooring. Cardinal Cushing of Boston dedicated it in August 1965, and a chapel commemorates the late President John F. Kennedy of the United States. The salmon weir is

one of the most unusual and popular of sights, as in season huge shoals of salmon can be seen queueing up to leap their way upstream to their mysterious spawning grounds. The nearby Franciscan Abbey, in Francis Street, is built on the site of the friary founded in 1296 by William Liath de Burgo.

The Lynch Memorial, near the Church of St Nicholas, is a built-up Gothic door, above which, set in the black marble, is the inscripton, 'This memorial of the stern and unbending justice of the chief magistrate of this City, James Lynch FitzStephen,

Padraic O'Conaire atop his throne of rubble in Eyre Square

The Spanish Arch was built in Galway in 1594

elected Mayor A.D. 1493 who condemned and executed his own guilty son, Walter on this spot.' Beneath this, on a stone dated 1624, is the inscription, 'Remember Death. Vanite of Vanites, Al is Vanite.' Tradition says that Walter ran his sword through a young Spanish visitor who was 'on their Keeping', in a duel over a girl, and as nobody else in the city would carry out the sentence of death, Judge Lynch hanged his own son from a window of the house.

The Allied Irish Bank in Shop Street occupies the fine old building of Lynch's Castle, a family mansion dating from 1320. The walls are beautifully decorated with coats of arms and carved stone work, and the fireplaces date from Henry VIII's time. Similar buildings and shops are to be found in Shop Street, Abbeygate Street, St Augustine Street and Middle Street. In the centre of the city is the John Fitzgerald Kennedy Memorial Park, in honour of the late President of the United States, who spoke to the people of Galway in June 1983 from the spot now marked with a memorial plaque. In the Square stands the

Browne doorway, and the charmingly playful stone statue to the Irish scholar and short-story writer, Padraic O'Conaire (1883-1928). The statue is by Albert Power R.H.A.

In the Bank of Ireland, at 19 Eyre Square, the 17th-century Galway Silver Sword and the Great Mace of 1710 are on display.

The Spanish Arch, and Spanish Parade, are all that remain of the 1594 wall of arches to protect the Spanish ships unloading their cargoes.

The Galway City Museum at the Spanish Arch covers all aspects of life and the city's history. The Claddagh, on the West bank of the River Corrib, was for many years an Irish speaking fishing village of thatched cottages with its own first citizen or 'King'. The Claddagh ring, the traditional wedding ring of Galway, a heart held between two hands, is a popular souvenir of the city.

University College Galway, an old 'Queen's University', built in 1845, in Tudor style, is now very much a Gaelic University and much used by American student summer schools. Millions of pounds exchange hands through the bookies at the celebrated annual Galway Races held July/August at Ballybrit Race track.

GALWAY CITY is 135 miles west of Dublin.

KILMACDUAGH
County Galway

Because it is very much off the map, visitors making the effort to see this monastic settlement of the 6th-century St Colman will probably find themselves sharing the view with only a flock of sheep. It has a collection

Kylemore Abbey delights the eye, a fairytale mansion above a lake

of assorted churches and a round tower, 112 ft high, known as the Irish 'Leaning Tower of Pisa' as it is really leaning over two feet off its perpendicular line! The cathedral building is 14th century, 98 ft long, and contains the altar-tomb of the O'Shaughnessys.

KILMACDUAGH is 3 miles south west of Gort.

KYLEMORE
County Galway

Kylemore Abbey, north of Clifden, and on one of the most beautiful scenic routes through the 12 Bens of Connemara, is a glorious castellated mansion standing on the shores of Kylemore Lake. Once the home of Mitchell Henry, an M.P. of the 1860s, it is now a convent and school of the Irish Benedictine nuns of Ypres. It has charming tea rooms and an excellent souvenir shop with first class pottery. The Gothic chapel is beautifully furnished with Connemara marble.

KYLEMORE is less than 10 miles north west of Clifden.

LOUGHREA
County Galway

Loughrea – *Baile Locha Riach* – Grey Lough Town, is an attractive market town, beautifully situated on the north side of a lake, famous for its coarse fish angling. The town was founded by the Norman, Richard de Burg, in 1300. He established the Carmelite Priory, the remains of which are still to be seen in the middle of the town, but its main attraction is St Brendan's Cathedral, not because of its dull exterior, but because of the exciting, artistic content of its interior. There are superb examples of Irish stained glass work of the incomparable Evie Hone, A.E.

Exquisite stained glass in the cathedral at Loughrea

Child, Michael Healy, Hubert McGoldrick, Sarah Purser, Patrick Pye and Ethel Rhind. There are embroideries by Jack Yeats and sculptures by John Hughes, notably in the Lady Chapel. The artworks span the period from around 1900-1950, and were greatly inspired and assisted by Edward Martyn (1859-1923) of Galway, who was the inspiration behind the Irish stained glass revival movement.

Just two miles north of Loughrea is the Turoe Stone, the finest example in Ireland of La Tene Celtic art. It is a phallic symbol, connected with some ancient pagan ritual, 3 ft high, and covered in a profusion of Celtic curvilinear designs and a Greek step outline. It is related to similar stones in Ireland and in Brittany, and dates from 100 BC.

🚗 *LOUGHREA is 22 miles east of Galway and 19 miles west of Ballinasloe.*

PORTUMNA FOREST PARK
County Galway

The old town of Portumna — 'The Oak Harbour' — looks out over Lough Derg, and makes a bridge across the River Shannon. Just outside the town are the impressive ruins of Portumna Castle, once the home of Lord Clanricarde, one of the lesser-loved landlords of the area.

Adjacent to the town is Portumna Forest Park, 1403 superb acres of recreational and amenity land all along the edge of Lough Derg. Complete with a wildlife sanctuary, with hides for birdwatching, and a herd of fallow deer, it has fine nature trails.

The large harbour is a haven for mooring boats and cruisers on the mighty River Shannon.

🚗 *PORTUMNA FOREST PARK is 20 miles from Ballinashoe and 24 miles by river from Killaloe.*

ROSSERK ABBEY
County Mayo

Founded around 1400 by one of the Joyce Clan, Rosserk Abbey is a Franciscan friary, and one of the best preserved typical friary churches in the country. Look closely at the double piscina and you will see the carving of an early Celtic round tower.

🚗 *ROSSERK ABBEY is 4 miles north of Ballina.*

THOOR BALLYLEE
County Galway

Thoor Ballylee, a Norman square tower, was originally the home of Richard de Burg in the 16th century. William Butler Yeats purchased it for £35, fully restored it, and used it on and off as his ivory tower during the early 1920s. When the castle fell back into ruins after he moved to Dublin, the Irish Tourist Board fully restored it as a four-storey precious national monument, open to the public, and with a erudite and cultured guide in charge. The original oak furniture, designed by W.A. Scott, the china, some first editions of Yeats, and all the colourful broadsheets of his brother, Jack, are on view. Yeats' 'Winding stair, a chamber arched with stone. A grey stone fireplace with an open hearth,' are still there, in situ, and there is a marvellous view from the flat roof of the tower. Splendid teas and conversation are to be had in the adjacent Yeatsian thatched cottage.

🚗 *THOOR BALLYLEE is 3 miles north east of Gort on the Galway-Ennis road.*

WESTPORT
County Mayo

Westport, on the edge of the vastness that is Clew Bay, 15 miles

long and six miles wide, has the unique distinction of being a town that was designed by James Wyatt. Westport House, designed in 1731 by Richard Castle with additions by James Wyatt, was the first stately home in Ireland to open its doors to the public. It is run by Jeremy Ulick, 12th Earl of Altamont and his wife Jennifer. Richard Castle built it for the 1st Earl, and it has remained in the family ever since. A family of engaging eccentrics, the Lord Sligo of 1812, friend of Byron, excavated and brought back to Westport from his 'Grand Tour' the 3000 year old columns that guarded the Treasury of Atreus at Mycenae, the tomb of Agamemnon. They were later presented to the British museum, the concrete substitute columns now adorn the home. There is a magnificent entrance hall with a Sicilian marble staircase. To the left of the entrance is the library designed by James Wyatt. The drawing room to the right incorporates wood from the Lord Sligo estates in Jamaica. The house is full of panelled walls, magnificent plaster ceilings, old Irish silver, Waterford glass and rare furniture. There are statues by Antonio Rossetti and John Gibson, and, notably a Mother and Child by Dalou. There is a Chinese room, a gallery of landscapes, and family protraits by Kneller, Reynolds and Copley. The dining room is by James Wyatt's son, Benjamin. On the premises are tea rooms, caravan and camping parks, a zoo park and a children's playground.

WESTPORT is 162 miles from Dublin, and 52 miles north west of Galway.

Each room in Westport House is furnished in elegant style

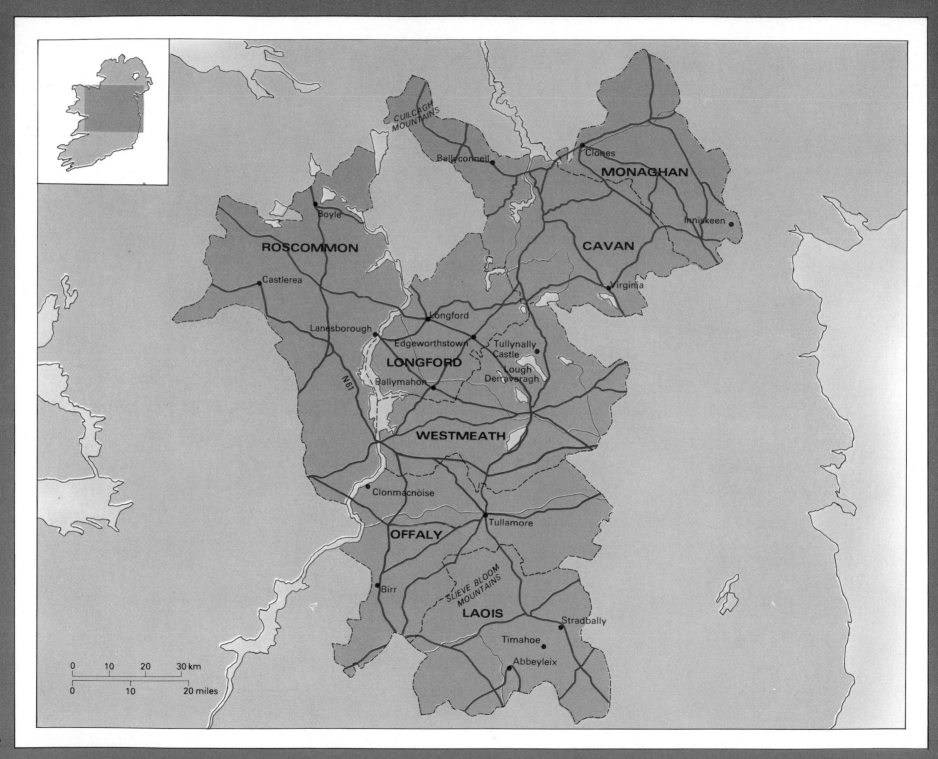

CUILCAGH
MOUNTAINS

Ballyconnell

Clones

MONAGHAN

Boyle

ROSCOMMON

CAVAN

Inniskeen

Castlerea

Virginia

Longford

Lanesborough

Edgeworthstown

Tullynally
Castle

N61

LONGFORD

Lough
Derravaragh

Ballymahon

WESTMEATH

Clonmacnoise

Tullamore

OFFALY

Birr

SLIEVE BLOOM
MOUNTAINS

LAOIS

Stradbally

Timahoe

Abbeyleix

0   10   20   30 km

0   10   20 miles

Cavan is a lakeland county, embracing the source of the mighty River Shannon and a scattering of beautiful lakes such as this, Lough Sheelin at Mount Nugent

A GULL'S EYE VIEW of the Midlands shows Athlone, County Westmeath, right in the middle of Ireland, on the River Shannon, which divides the Province of Leinster from Connacht. Offaly is famous for the home of the Earl and Countess of Rosse, Birr Castle, with its superb gardens, open to the public, incorporating 100 acres of 1000 different species of trees and shrubs. To the south is Laois, formerly Queen's County, named after Queen Mary in the reign of Philip and Mary. Westmeath, to the north of Offaly is fat cattle pasture land. It is Goldsmith country, as he was born at Pallas or Elphin in 1730. Edgeworthstown is famous as the home, still standing today, of the novelist, Maria Edgeworth (1768-1849) whose writings inspired Turgenev and Sir Walter Scott. Roscommon, north west of Athlone, is lakeland country, embracing the vast waters of the beautiful Lough Ree. Longford is forever associated with the late Lord Longford, patron of the Gate Theatre in Dublin, and Frank Pakenham, now Lord Longford. The family mansion, (open to the public) Tullynally Castle, is actually in County Westmeath. It is a remarkable 'gothic' castle, once the home of Kitty Pakenham who married the Duke of Wellington. Cavan, the most southerly of the nine counties of Ulster, is a lakeland of amazing beauty, and the Shannon 'Pot' has its source at Cuilcagh. Its source is so small that you can almost leap across it!

93

94 **Abbeyleix House stands in woodland gardens laid down by Emma, wife of the third Viscount de Vesci**

ABBEYLEIX
County Laois

Abbeyleix – *Mainistear Laoighse* – the Abbey of Laoighis, takes its name from the now long-since vanished Cistercian monastery founded in 1183 by Conor O'More. Today the attractive, tree-lined town is dominated by the Viscount de Vesci stately home designed by James Wyatt in 1773, and built by William Chambers for Thomas, the first Viscount de Vesci. While the house is not open to the public the magnificent woodland gardens which surround the house are. They contain a superb collection of giant oaks, natives of the woods, supplemented by rare and exotic specimens of ornamental trees, shrubs and flowers. Within the walls, in the King's Garden, is the tomb of the Prince of Laois, Malachy O'More, who died in 1486, and the 13th-century monk's bridge over the River Nore is still in use, all that is left of the original 12th-century Cistercian monastery.
🚗 *ABBEYLEIX is 60 miles south west of Dublin and 9 miles south of Port Laoise.*

BALLYCONNELL
County Cavan

Ballyconnell, a pretty town on the Cavan-Fermanagh border, has twice won the coveted National Tidy Towns Award. It lies at the foot of Slieve Russell (1331 ft) and the Cuilcagh Mountain (2188 ft). It is a superb coarse fishing centre, and gets its name from Conal Cearnach, the 1st-century Red Branch Knight who slew the King of Connacht, and was slain in revenge by the King's men. On the western slope of Cuilcagh Mountain is the little-known 'Shannon Pot', the source of the mightiest and longest river in these islands. It is a marshy spot on the mountainside, and the temptation is to leap across the welling waters and their surrounding shrubs, to boast that you have leapt across the Shannon. However, common sense should prevail as you would really need to be an Olympic Gold Medalist to succeed. The views from this spot on the Cavan-Fermanagh border are extremely beautiful. At Killycluggin, just three miles to the south west of Ballyconnell, is a phallic stone with Celtic designs, similar to the Turoe Stone of County Galway. This is pagan country, as it was in this neighbourhood that

St Patrick overthrew the druidic idol of Crom Crúaich, on the 'Plain of Adoration'.

BALLYCONNELL is 8 miles north of Killeshandra and 7 miles west of Belturbet.

BALLYMAHON
County Longford

Ballymahon – literally 'Mahon's Town' – is named after Mahon, King of Thomond, who defeated Fergal, son of Ruarc, High King of Bréifne and Connacht here in 960. Beautifully situated on the charming River Inny, the river is spanned here by a five arch bridge from which you can

see the brown trout in the river below.

This is the very heart of the Goldsmith country as the essayist, poet and playwright was born near here, at Pallas, five miles north of the town. A statue to him was unveiled in Pallas in 1974 to mark his bi-centenary year. Goldsmith (1728-1774), fully earned his epitaph that 'nothing touched that he did not adorn'. His novel *The Vicar of Wakefield* was widely aclaimed, his poem *The Deserted Village* established him, and his play *She Stoops to Conquer* immortalised him.

Auburn, just six miles from Pallas, where Goldsmith went to

school, and his father was rector, (its real name is Lissoy) is referred to as 'Sweet Auburn' in his *Deserted Village*. A little to the north-east is the Three Jolly Pigeons pub, named after the Inn in *She Stoops To Conquer*. Its doorstep is the mill stone from the 'Busy Mill' with its 'never failing brook'. The ruins of the Ale house, 'where village statesmen talked and looked profound', still remain. The front wall and the end walls of the original Lissoy Parsonage still stand.

Ardagh, a sweet little village three miles south-west of Edgeworthstown, is where Goldsmith mistook Ardagh House for an inn and used the incident in the plot of *She Stoops To Conquer*. His statue by John Henry Foley, stands in College Green outside the College of the Holy and Undivided Trinity, where he was educated. All the places associated with Goldsmith are well signposted.

BALLYMAHON is 69 miles from Dublin and 13 miles from Longford.

BIRR
County Offaly

Birr Castle, home of the Earl and Countess of Rosse, is famous for its beautiful demesne gardens, open to the public. The 100-acre grounds cover 1000 different species of shrubs and trees. In spring the formal gardens are a mass of flowering magnolia, and in autumn the maples and hedges are magnificent. There are hornbeam walks, and the box hedges are the tallest in the world. In the grounds are the remains of the Great Telescope invented by the 3rd Earl of Rosse (1800-1867) with which he mapped the milky way and discovered the spiral nebulae. Another exhibition commemorates

Twice winner of the Tidy Towns Award, Ballyconnell also boasts the mysterious Tomregon Stone

Sir Charles Parsons (1854-1931) the youngest son of the 3rd Earl of Rosse, who invented the steam turbine. He put the fear of God into the entire coal-burning British Navy, assembled before the King for review at Spithead, when he darted in and out of the fleet in his fast steam turbine powered boat.

Anthony Armstrong Jones and Princess Margaret were frequent visitors to Birr Castle, as the Countess of Rosse is the mother of Princess Margaret's former husband.

BIRR is 27 miles south of Athlone and 80 miles south west of Dublin.

BOYLE
County Roscommon

Boyle – 'The Monastery of the Pasture River' – lies at the foot of the Curlew Mountains on the north bank of the River Boyle which links Lough Gara with Lough Key.

Two miles to the north east of Boyle is Lough Key Forest Park, a lovely wild park where the Departments of Fisheries, Tourism and Forest and Wildlife have combined to make a natural wonderland of forest walks, boating and swimming. There is an excellent lakeside restaurant. Lough Gara, just west of Boyle, is an area rich in antiquities dating from 2500 BC, with over 300 crannogs, over 30 dug-out boats, and one of the largest dolmens in Ireland, 15 ft long and 11 ft wide on five standing stones.

BOYLE is 117 miles from Dublin and 27 miles north of Roscommon.

BOYLE ABBEY
County Roscommon

The Cistercian Abbey of Boyle was established in 1161 by Abbot Maurice O'Duffy and was closely linked with

The stately grey pile of Birr Castle is surrounded by glorious grounds

the great Abbey of Mellifont in County Louth. It was partially destroyed in 1569, but retains its massive and picturesque ruins of a cruciform church, a lofty central tower, and a large nave, choir, kitchen and cloisters.

BOYLE ABBEY is in the town of Boyle, 25 miles from Sligo and 117 from Dublin.

CASTLE LESLIE
County Monaghan

Castle Leslie, originally a medieval fortress, is today the 1870s stately home of the distinguished Leslie family. In its grounds there is one of the finest equestrian cross-country courses in these islands.

One branch of the family was connected with the mother of Sir Winston Churchill, and they still have his baby dress! Charles Powell Leslie paid for the upbringing of his brother-in-law, Lord Mornington, who was without means, and who later became Duke of Wellington. His Waterloo bridle and death mask are preserved in the castle.

CASTLE LESLIE is at Glaslough, 7 miles north east of the town of Monaghan.

CASTLEREA
County Roscommon

Castlerea – 'The Grey Castle' – is a pretty wooden village on the River Suck, which was the birthplace of Sir William Wilde (1815-1876), an eminent Dublin eye specialist and antiquarian and father of Oscar Wilde (1854-1900), dramatist and wit. Sir William's wife, Lady Wilde (1826-1896) wrote patriotic verse and articles for the *Nation*, the newspaper voice of the Young Ireland Movement, under the pen name of 'Speranza'.

Just west of the town is Clonalis

Boyle Abbey is magnificent even in its ruined state

House, the ancestral home of the Clan of Connacht, who ruled the province and produced the High Kings of Ireland, notably Turlough Mor who died in 1156. Arguably the oldest documented family in Europe, their genealogical papers go back over 1500 years. This Victorian House, set in parkland, is a treasure house of ancient Irish manuscripts, books, documents, regalia, costume, furniture and paintings, open to the public. The portraits include the pictures of Major Owen O'Connor, Count and Countess O'Rourke, and Don Carlos O'Connor. Count O'Rourke, father of Bishop O'Rourke, was killed fighting the red-coats of Marlborough at the Bat-

tle of Luzzara. His wife was Maid-of-Honour at the Court of King James, in France. The O'Connors fought as brigadiers and high ranking officers in the 'Wild Geese' Irish regiments in the service of France, and in the Regiment of Dillon. In the dining room is a portrait of Don Carlos O'Connor, Spanish Diplomat. The portrait of Charles O'Connor of New York shows the man who was the first Catholic ever to have been nominated to the Presidency of the United States. He was defeated by Ulysses Grant in 1872. Clonalis House is open to the public.

CASTLEREA is 19 miles north of Roscommon.

CLONES
County Monaghan

Clones was the site of a monastery founded by St Tighearnach who died in AD 548. The 10th-century Celtic Cross of the Scriptures, 15 ft high, formally stood near the Round Tower, and now stands in the town square. The Round Tower in the graveyard is 75 ft in height with a square headed doorway. The adjacent shrine of St Tighearnach is in the shape of a house carved out of a single stone. All around this area are superb coarse fishing lakes. The town is famous for its lace making.

CLONES is 13 miles south west of Monaghan town.

CLONMACNOISE
County Offaly

"In a quiet watered land, a land
of roses,
Stands Saint Kieran's city fair;
And the warriors of Erin in their
famous generations
Slumber there ...
There they laid to rest the seven
Kings of Tara
There the sons of Cairbre sleep
Battle-banners of the Gael that
in Kieran's plain of crosses
Now their final hosting keep..."

Thus wrote the poet T.W. Rolleston (1857-1920), translating the Irish of Angus O'Gillan, about the mighty monastic city of Clonmacnoise on the banks of the Shannon, city of churches, high crosses and round towers, founded by St Kieran in AD 548 and which flourished for over 1000 years. Entering the monastic enclosure from the car park there are ten churches, two round towers, a castle, three high crosses, including the superb 10th-century 'Cross of the Scriptures' and over 400 historic gravestones and tomb stones.

🚗 CLONMACNOISE is 4 miles north of Shannonbridge. The ideal approach is 9 miles by river from Athlone.

Clonmacnoise (seen from the air, left) is full of ancient monastic remains like the ones below

DÚN A RÍ FOREST PARK
County Cavan

Dún a Rí Forest Park covers 588 acres and part of the famous Kingscourt Forest. It is noted for its mixed hardwoods and conifers. It has an excellent selection of nature trails.

🚗 DÚN A RÍ PARK is 1 mile north of Kingscourt on the road to Carrickmacross.

EDGEWORTHSTOWN
County Longford

Edgeworthstown is a delightful market town. It takes its name from the Edgeworth family, formerly of Edgeworthstown House, a Georgian house, later a convent, and now a nursing home, built by Richard Lovell Edgeworth (1744-1817) author, inventor and father of the novelist Maria Edgeworth (1767-1849). Maria achieved fame with her novel *Castle Rackrent*, first published in 1800. She influenced the writings of Turgenev and entertained Sir Walter Scott, whose novels she also influenced, and also William Wordsworth, in her Longford home. Their family vault is in the local Protestant church, in which the delightful Maria Edgeworth Museum is housed. Her novels were published in 12 volumes. Another famous Edgeworth was the Abbé Edgeworth de Firmont, (Firmont is a village three miles north of Edgeworthstown), son of Essex Edgeworth, who was confessor to Louis XVI at his death on the scaffold.

🚗 EDGEWORTHSTOWN is 69 miles north west of Dublin and 19 miles north west of Mullingar.

EMO COURT
County Laois

Emo Court, a private residence, is a glorious house designed in 1790 by James Gandon, who also designed the Church of Ireland church in Coolbanagher, two and a half miles south of Emo. Formerly a Jesuit Novitiate, Emo Court has magnificent gardens with fine specimens of trees and shrubs, open to the public by special arrangement.

🚗 EMO COURT is 45 miles from Dublin off the main Dublin to Cork and Limerick road.

INNISKEEN
County Monaghan

In the local Folk Museum in this charming village, is a section devoted to the poet Patrick Kavanagh (1904-1967), who was born in the vicinity and worked as a cobbler and small farmer. While working here he published his first collection of poems *The Ploughman and Other Poems* in 1936. In his two light semi-autobiographical novels *The Green Fool* and *Tarry Flynn* he described life during the 'thirties in the tiny village. His actual birthplace was the adjacent townland of Muckner, and he lies buried in the local cemetery. The remains of a Round Tower in Inniskeen show that it was once the monastic settlement of the 6th-century St Dega.

🚗 INNISKEEN is 7 miles north east of Carrickmacross.

Patrick Kavanagh

The seven counties, roughly grouped together into their collective 'Midlands', have in their midst a major poet who binds them together, Patrick Kavanagh, the 'ploughman poet' (1904-1967) who was born and farmed for 30 years in Iniskeen in the 'hungry hills' of Monaghan. Arguably the greatest Irish poet since W.B. Yeats, he caught the spirit of childhood as he looked back from his adult days of quiet desperation. The poet who is,

"...astonished
At a stick carried down a stream
Or at the undying difference in the corner of a field"

and who remembers so vividly

"...the newness that was in every stale thing
When we looked at it as children;"
Or the prophetic astonishment in the tedious talking

"Of an old fool ...
... the bog-holes, cart tracks, old stables where time begins."

In his poem, *Shancoduff*, the midland counties share in this image,

"My hills hoard the bright shillings of March
While the sun searches in every pocket."

And the bog-lands shared by these regions are reflected thus;

"That beautiful, beautiful beautiful God
Was breathing his love by a cut-away bog."

In his poem, *Peace* he asks:

"Out of that childhood country what fools climb
To fight with tyrants Love and Life and Time?"

Lake Derravaragh — Kavanagh was inspired by melancholy Midland beauty such as this

KILLY KEEN FOREST PARK
County Cavan

Killy Keen Forest Park comprises 600 acres of spectacular beauty. Its Devinish nature trail takes in a number of crannogs, or ancient lakeside dwelling places, the most notable being that of Cloughoughter. There are four excellent fishing locations beside the lake, and a car park.

Cloughoughter Castle, the remains of which still stand on a small island in Lough Oughter, was once the 13th-century fortress of the O'Reilly's.

🚗 *KILLY KEEN FOREST PARK is 8 miles west of the town of Cavan.*

LANESBOROUGH
County Longford

Lanesborough, a delightful town spanning the River Shannon, with a nine arch bridge at the tip of the northern end of Lough Ree, is a Shannon River cruising centre. Lough Ree is a coarse fish angler's paradise, and the Shannon at this point is a trout fisherman's heaven. A glimpse of modern Ireland can be seen near the town on the east bank in the form of a turf-fired electricity generating power station. On the island of Lough Ree is the 6th-century monastery founded by St Diarmuid, who taught St Kieran of Clonmacnoise. The history of the island is much older than this as there are great Ogham stones and a small circular mound said to have been the Palace of Queen Maeve. The legend concerning her is unkind to the men of Ulster, as it claims that one of their number took a shot at her with a stone from a sling, and killed her while she was bathing!

🚗 *LANESBOROUGH is 19 miles by boat or 27 miles by road from Athlone.*

LONGFORD
County Longford

The town of Longford – from the Irish word for 'fortress', lies on the southern bank of the charming River Camlin, east of the mighty River Shannon. Nothing is left of the original ancient O'Farrell Fortress, princes of Annaly, after which the town was named. The enormous St Mel's Cathedral dominates the town. At the rear of the cathedral is the Diocesan Museum, open to the public, (admission free), which houses the crozier of St Mel, the shrine of St Manchan and much of the library from Edgeworthstown House, the former home of the novelist, Maria Edgeworth. At Clondra, seven miles west of the handsome town, is the village's *Teach Cheoil* or Irish Music House, where the best of old-fashioned Irish music can be heard in traditional kitchen-like surroundings.

🚗 *LONGFORD is 8¼ miles north west of Edgeworthstown.*

LOUGH DERRAVARAGH
County Westmeath

County Westmeath boasts three beautiful lakes; the picturesque Lough Ennell, six miles long and three miles wide, Lough Owel, 2200 acres of brown trout fishing, and Lough Derravaragh – 'The Lake of the Oaks' – with its well wooded shores and waters teeming with trout, pike and perch. However, the greatest attraction of its shining waters is that it is the scene of the most tragic of all Irish romantic legends, 'The Fate of the Children of Lir'. Lir was the Tuatha Dé Danann Chief whose second wife, Aoife, a witch, was so jealous of her four step-children that she changed them into swans, and decreed that they would remain so until the sound of the first Mass bell in Ireland. The whole Irish saga is a metaphor for the freeing of Ireland from the pagan bondage of the Druids. And so it was, after 900 years of suffering, that the magic spell ceased at the sound of St Patrick's Mass bell, and the children Finola, Aedh, Fiachra and Conn returned to their human form, and were converted and baptised by St Mochaomhog.

LOUGH DERRAVARAGH is approximately 4 miles south west of Castlepollard.

ROSSMORE FOREST PARK
County Monaghan

Rossmore Forest Park is 691 acres of woodland set among pleasant hills and tiny lakes just south and adjacent to the town of Monaghan.

Formerly it was the estate of the Cunningham family, the first holder of the Rossmore baronetcy title being General Robert Cunningham, MP for Monaghan from 1769 to 1796.

It has a number of nature trails and carefully laid out forest walks.

ROSSMORE FOREST PARK is next door to Monaghan town which is 17 miles from Armagh, and 75 from Dublin.

STRADBALLY
County Laois

Stradbally is a charming little 17th-century town which is historically the centre of the Clan O'More, the O'Mores of Noughaval who, for centuries, had in their possession the precious 'Book of Leinster'. The town boasts the Stradbally Steam Museum, open to the public, and dedicated to the part played by steam in the social history of Ireland. A Steam Rally is held every August. Also open to the public is the Pony Stud, at Stradbally Hall. The 18th-century gardens of Stradbally Hall are well worth visiting for their unique herbaceous borders and 90 species of perennials.

Near Stradbally, on the road to Portlaoise, is the Rock of Dunamase.

STRADBALLY is 9 miles from Athy and 7 miles from Portlaoise.

The Rock of Dunamase is a Celtic fortress symbolising the struggle for territorial possession in the Midlands

TIMAHOE
County Laois

Timahoe – *Teach Mo-Chúa* – the House of Mo-Chua, named after St Mochua who died in 657, boasts a fine 11th-century Round Tower 96 ft high, and with a base circumference of 57 ft, the largest of any Round Tower in Ireland. It is made from local limestone and sandstone and is divided into a basement and five storeys. One of the unique features is the fine Romanesque doorway, 17 ft above the ground. It is splendidly ornamented with little bearded heads.

The Catholic church in Timahoe has two magnificent stained glass windows by Michael Healy (1873-1941) who was one of the original stained glass artists of *An Túr Gloine*, which he joined in 1903. *TIMAHOE is 7½ miles south east of Portlaoise.*

TULLAMORE
County Offaly

The town of Tullamore – *Tulac Mór* the Great Assembly Hill, was once the mound of ancient formal assemblies but is now famous as the home of the Irish Mist Liqueur Company, the leading liqueur made in Ireland with 100 years of history. The factory welcomes visitors. Admission is free. *TULLAMORE is 60 miles west of Dublin.*

TULLYNALLY CASTLE
County Westmeath

Tullynally Castle, formerly Pakenham Hall, is the residence of the celebrated literary family, the Longfords, and is open to the public. Lord Longford's son, Tom Pakenham, is the present owner. Ed-

mund Pakenham came to Ireland as secretary to Sir Henry Sidney, Queen Elizabeth's Lord Deputy. Henry, his grandson, purchased Tullynally in 1655. Neighbour Richard Lovell Edgeworth, the inventor, installed gas-fired, underfloor central heating around 1794, the first in these islands! The house was made into a 'Gothic' castle between 1801 and 1806 by Francis Johnson, to make it look like an Irish version of Inveraray Castle in Scotland. It was a fortress during the 1798 insurrection. The ground plan of this romantic castle shows it to be nearly 400 ft long. There is a huge front hall, complete with organ, a vast bow-windowed drawing room, a charming library, a family wing, and a huge Victorian kitchen installed by the bachelor third Earl, who obviously enjoyed his food and being waited on by masses of servants. The latest addition to the castle is the 1860 Gothic tower by the architect of the late Lord Mountbatten's Castle, Classiebawn in County Sligo. Kitty Pakenham married the Duke of Wellington and the house is full of fascinating family history. The present Lord Longford, under the name of Frank Pakenham, wrote the definitive book on the Irish Troubles, *Peace by Ordeal*. Lady Elizabeth Longford is famous as a writer of historical biographies, notably her life of the Duke of Wellington. Tom Pakenham is the author of a history of the 1798 Rebellion, *The Year of Liberty*, and a study of the Boer War. The 6th Earl of Longford (1902-1961) was a director of the Gate Theatre and founder of Longford Productions. *TULLYNALLY CASTLE is 1½ miles west of Castlepollard.*

Tullynally Castle's sturdy facade

VIRGINIA
County Cavan

Virginia, a market town on the banks of lovely Lough Ramor, five miles of beautiful wooded shores and waters, is named after the 'Virgin Queen', Elizabeth I. Three miles north of the town is Cuilcagh Lough, on whose banks once stood Cuilcagh House, the home of schoolmaster the Reverend Thomas Sheridan (1687-1738) friend of Dean Jonathan Swift who began writing *Gulliver's Travels* here. Thomas Sheridan was the father of another Thomas Sheridan, actor-manager of Smock Alley Theatre, Dublin, and grandfather of Richard Brinsley Sheridan (1751-1816) playwright, immortalised by his works *The Rivals* and *The School for Scandal*.

Ballyjamesduff, a town just six miles north west of Virginia, was made famous in a song by Percy French, *Come Back Paddy Reilly*. It was also the birthplace of William James, who emigrated to America in 1789 and was the grandfather of William James the philosopher, and of the novelist, Henry James.

VIRGINIA is 52 miles from Dublin.

Virginia is beautifully laid out on the banks of Lough Ramor

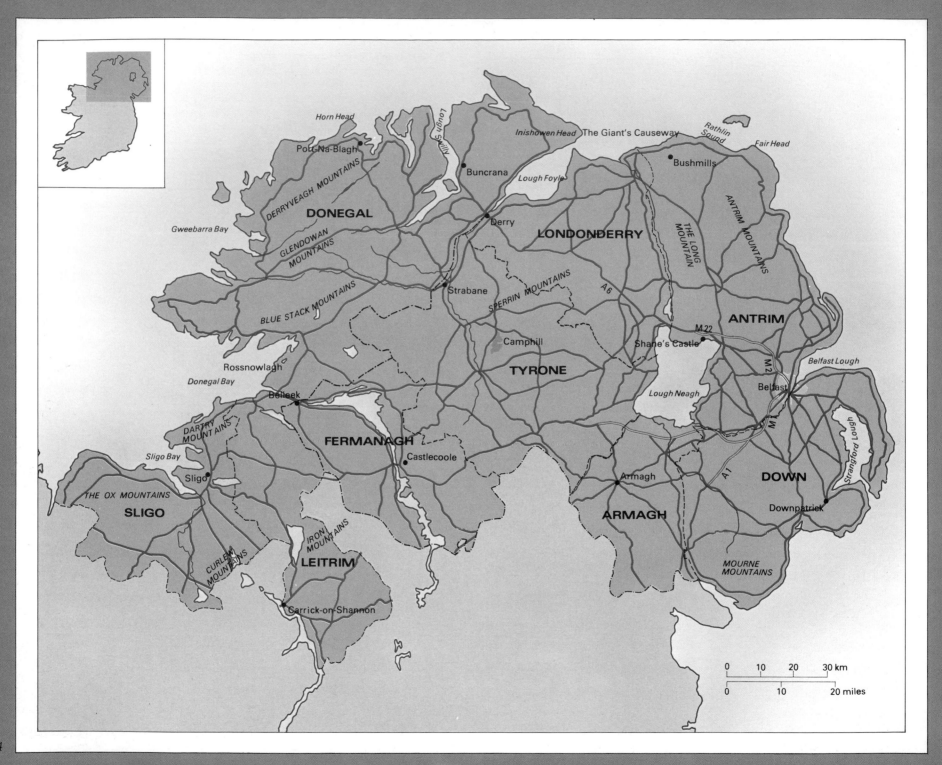

Horn Head

Pott-Na-Blagh

Lough Swilly

Inishowen Head The Giant's Causeway

Rathlin Sound

Buncrana

Fair Head

Bushmills

DONEGAL

Derryveagh Mountains

Lough Foyle

ANTRIM MOUNTAINS

Gweebarra Bay

Derry

LONDONDERRY

THE LONG MOUNTAIN

GLENDOWAN MOUNTAINS

Strabane

Sperrin Mountains

A6

ANTRIM

BLUE STACK MOUNTAINS

M 22

Camphill

Shane's Castle

M 2

Rossnowlagh

TYRONE

Belfast Lough

Donegal Bay

Belleek

Lough Neagh

Belfast

DARTRY MOUNTAINS

FERMANAGH

Strangford Lough

Sligo Bay

Castlecoole

A 1

DOWN

Sligo

Armagh

THE OX MOUNTAINS

SLIGO

ARMAGH

Downpatrick

IRON MOUNTAINS

CURLEW MOUNTAINS

LEITRIM

MOURNE MOUNTAINS

Carrick-on-Shannon

| 0 | 10 | 20 | 30 km |
| 0 | | 10 | 20 miles |

The ancient Irish were convinced that County Antrim's Giant's Causeway was the work of Ulster warrior-giant Finn McCool. In fact, this mass of basalt columns, mostly hexagonal, is the result of volcanic action

THE REGION WE CALL 'The North' transcends all man-made political lines, and flows fully and naturally across the Atlantic coastline of Sligo, Leitrim and Donegal, swinging around the stepping stones to Scotland of Derry, Antrim and Down, embracing the vast lakeland that is Fermanagh and the glory of the O'Neill territories of Tyrone. A tidy people these Northerners, they have gathered together all their industrial might in one place, Belfast, leaving the unspoilt countryside and the clean sandy beaches, the massive lakes and rivers free. The countryside and new forests are as neat and tidy as the kit of an Irish guardsman laid out for inspection! The Northern Irish are largely made up of hard working small farmers, with a scattering of great 'garrison' houses of the old Etonian guardsmen, who kept the British army supplied with leaders, men such as Alexander of Tunis, Governor General of Canada. Irish soldiers such as Lord Terence O'Neill of Shane's Castle, Prime Minister of Northern Ireland from 1963 to 1969. The 'Micks', the Irish Guards, where would they be without them? Some dozen great houses remain, run by the National Trust, and open to the public. Ardress and the Argory and Derrymore, in Armagh, Castlecoole and the Florence Court in Fermanagh, Castle Ward, Mount Stewart House and Rowallane Gardens in Down, Hazlett House, Springhill, and Mussenden Temple in Derry. Here, too, are the 'Northern Lights' of Irish literature and poetry.

ARMAGH
County Armagh

Armagh – *Ara Maca* – Macha's Height, was named after the fabulous warrior Queen, Macha, who founded the enormous fort of *Eamhain Macha* just two miles west of Armagh. Her burial place here dates from 300 BC, and *Eamhain Macha* was the seat of the Kings of Ulster from then until A.D. 332. Then King Conor MacNessa made it the training camp for his Red Branch Knights. The Church of Ireland Cathedral occupies the site of the original church of St Patrick. The Catholic Cathedral, twin towered, atop the hill, is 1840s Gothic, and here resides the Catholic Cardinal Archbishop of Armagh 'Primate of all Ireland.' Armagh, amid its seven hills, dated as an episcopal see from A.D. 445.

ARMAGH is 85 miles from Dublin.

BELFAST
County Antrim

Belfast, capital of Northern Ireland, lies on the River Lagan. Industrial centre of the North, well known for its huge ship-building yards and the manufacture of aircraft, the city has a noble 19th-century City Hall, a beautifully-restored Opera House, and its own Queen's University, established in 1849. The Ulster Museum, in the Botanic Gardens, near the University, houses a fine collection of Irish antiquities, including the Downpatrick Gold Hoards, historic Irish silver, and a magnificent Art Gallery which includes the works of Sickert, Steer, Stanley Spencer and Francis Bacon. Of particular interest is the dazzling collection of treasures recovered by underwater divers from the wreck of the largest ship in the Spanish Armada, the *Gerona*, which was wrecked off the Giant's Causeway in 1588. The treasures were recovered in 1968.

The annual Belfast Festival, the biggest in Britain after Edinburgh, takes place at The Queen's University and its environs. An exhilarating mixture of music, theatre, satire, dance, comedy and mime, the autumn festival draws international performers such as Yehudi Menuhin, actors Anthony Quayle and Ian McKellen and musicians such as Cleo Laine and Johnny Dankworth.

BELFAST is 103 miles north of Dublin and 75 miles from Derry.

This aerial view of Belfast (right) shows the blue dome of the city hall, seen from Windsor House

Queen's University (below) has mullioned windows and a fine Tudor cloister

BELLEEK
County Fermanagh

Belleek china, the internationally famous white lustre finished pottery, is named after the town where it has been manufactured by hand since 1863. Originally local clays and water power were used. The highly ornamental glazed earthenware covers a wide range, from fragile translucent teacups and saucers to intricate designs for pots, plates and teapots, with platted, inter-woven basket-like exteriors. Statues too, and ornate candelabra are all part of the tradition. Early Belleek pottery is particularly valuable, and much sought after by American collectors. There are many elegant modern Celtic designs with the shamrock motif. You can see the master potters at work on the porcelain, and the 'Fettlers', the men who assemble the pieces for the fiery furnaces.

BELLEEK is on the Donegal-Fermanagh border 23 miles from Enniskillen.

This intricate 'basket weave' design characterises Belleek pottery

BUNCRANA
County Donegal

Buncrana, perched on the east side of the Inishowen Peninsular, on the **shores** of Lough Foyle, is sheltered by high mountains such as Slieve Snacht (2019 ft), and is a charming seaside resort. Just 11 miles south is the most impressive and awesome stone fortress in Ireland, the Grianan of Aileach. A unique circular stone fort standing over 800 ft high above Loughs Swilly and Foyle on Greenan Mountain, it is 77 ft in diameter, with walls 17 ft high and 13 ft thick. Built in 1700 BC, it was once the residence of the O'Neills, Kings of Ulster.

BUNCRANA is 161 miles from Dublin and 13 from Derry.

Carrick-on-Shannon has a popular marina

CAMPHILL
County Tyrone

The Ulster-American Folk Park at Camphill, made possible by the generosity of the descendants of Thomas Mellon, founder of the Pittsburg, Pennsylvania banking family, recreates the old world and the new world in an imaginative presentation of buildings and their contents which tell the story of the emigration of Ulster people to the United States of America. The Dr Mathew T. Mellon Building at the entrance to the Folk Park shows audio-visual representations of the mass migration. There is a Pine Walk from there to the splendidly re-created forge, to the Weaver's Cottage, the Meeting House, and the *pièce de resistance*, the actual Mellon homestead, the cottage in which Thomas Mellon was born on 3 February 1813. His family emigrated with him to America in 1818, but he never forgot his humble cottage birthplace, and he returned to see it in 1882. There is a magnificent viewpoint atop the hill above the Mellon Homestead. Back to the Schoolhouse, moved from its original site in Castletown, it was founded in 1790 and renewed in 1845, retaining its name as the local 'National School'.

Then there is the 'New World' of the Log Cabin, based on the Mellon family farmhouse in Pennsylvania, the Log Barn, the Smoke House for hickory chip or corn cob, curing of bacon and of venison, the Springhouse or Dairy, the Corncob or Granary, the Camp Meeting Site, the Poultry Exhibit and, to cap it all, a magnificent Conestoga Wagon of 1790, the type of wagon in which the Mellon family and hundreds of thousands of Ulster emigrants moved West. The Ulster-American Folk

Irish whiskey — created not made

At Bushmills, in County Antrim, is the world's first licensed distillery, founded in 1608. Here, they make 'Old Bushmills', a deluxe Irish whiskey of superb quality, set apart and unique because it is a blend of a single malt and a single grain. The malt whiskey comes from the Bushmills distillery, the grain from the sister distillery in Coleraine. The barley is grown locally, and the water comes from the distillery's own privately owned tributary of the River Bush, St Columb's Rill. Bushmills whiskey has always been made with this special water which rises in peaty ground and flows over basalt. The Irish word for whiskey (always spelt with an 'e'), is *Uisce Beatha*, meaning, 'the water of life.' They say that Bushmills whiskey is not made, it is 'created.' The three raw materials in the creation are malted barley, yeast and water.

The Old Bushmills Distillery, where whiskey is 'created'

The first stage is milling, the malt being screened to ensure purity and quality, and then milled, or ground. The next stage is mashing, the 'grist', or ground malt, being mashed or mixed with hot water, and allowed to settle in a cylindrical cast-iron vessel called a 'Mash Tun.' The starch in the ground malt becomes sugar. The 'Wort', or sugar and water, are drained through the perforated base of the Mash Tun into a vessel called the 'underback'. The Wort is cooled on its way to the fermenting vessel known as the 'washback', where yeast is fed to the sugar producing the 'wash' which is non alcoholic. Ten gallons of wash make one gallon of alcohol at proof strength. Then comes the distillation process in pot stills. The wash is heated in the first still. The alcohol vapour is collected as a distillate which is heated in the second still. Then come the 'feints', the distillate is separated into two parts, the heads and the tails, the stronger heads being distilled in a third still, the 'Spirit' still, the tails recycled.

The third distillate is sampled by the stillman and from the pure spirit running he selects only that portion with the desired character and flavour, which goes into the Spirit Receiver at a collecting strength of 45° proof. Oak casks receive the spirits reduced in strength by the addition of purified water, and maturing takes place, the best being up to 12 years old, Bushmills famous 'Black Label'.

Park is a major tourist attraction in the north of Ireland.

🚗 *CAMPHILL is a 26-acre site, on the River Strule midway between Newtonstewart to its north, and 4 miles from Omagh to its south. It is approximately 73 miles from Belfast, 34 from Derry and 119 from Dublin.*

CARRICK-ON-SHANNON
County Leitrim

Carrick-on-Shannon, on the mighty River Shannon, is the centre for marinas and flotillas of cruisers who come to explore the most beautiful and navigable stretch of the river. It is also the coarse-fishing angling centre of the county and is equally famous for trout fishing. They say 'Leitrim, God help us!' is the poorest county in Ireland, but its little known mountains and lakes, with Lough Allen seven miles long and three miles wide, is every bit as beautiful as the better-known landscape of its neighbouring Sligo. Its Lough Melvin is famous for its salmon and trout angling.

🚗 *CARRICK-ON-SHANNON is 101 miles from Dublin and 23 from Longford.*

CASTLECOOLE
County Fermanagh

Bordering the town of Enniskillen, in a 1500-acre wooded demesne is Castlecoole, once the seat of the Earls of Belmore, now in the care of the National Trust, and open to the public. It has been described as the perfect Georgian house in Grecian Style, built of imported Portland Stone. Designed by James Wyatt, it was built in the 1790s. The plaster work is by Joseph Rose. The six mantels are by the English sculptor Westmacott and there is an excellent collection of period furniture. In the parklands, on the lake, are a famous flock of greylag geese.

🚗 *CASTLECOOLE is approximately 112 miles from Dublin and 86 from Belfast.*

DERRY
County Derry

Derry – *Doire* – The Oak Wood, dates from the year 546 when St Colmcille, or Columba as he was more generally known, founded a monastery here. Tradition ascribes an ancient Irish verse to Colmcille, who expressed his love for his favourite monastery thus, 'Derry, my own grove, Little cell, my home, my love.' The Protestant Cathedral stands on the site of his monastery. It is a walled city, famous for its siege of 1689, and these walls today are a delightful promenade. Situated on the estuary of the River Foyle, it is the gateway to the romantic county of Donegal, which lies on its western side.

DERRY is 152 miles from Dublin, 75 miles from Belfast, and 25 from Letterkenny.

DOWNPATRICK
County Down

Downpatrick – *Dun Padraig* – St Patrick's Fort, is where St Patrick founded his first or second church, after his return to Ireland. The Church of Ireland Cathedral, standing at the western edge of the town, was built in the 1800s to include part of the 12th-century cathedral in its nave and transepts. Outside the east end of the cathedral is a re-assembled 10th-century Celtic cross. There is a large granite boulder in the churchyard on the south side of this cathedral, marked 'Patric', placed there in 1900, and, without any evidence, the reputed burial place of St Patrick. Excavations on this hill site in 1985 have simply uncovered evidence of a large medieval building and a very early Christian cemetery. Defensive ditches, and bronze age pottery 2500 years old have also been found.

Perfectly situated on the River Quoile, just three miles from Downpatrick, are the remains of Inch Abbey, a Cistercian foundation of John de Courcy in 1180, who brought over monks from Furness Abbey in Lancashire. Saul – *Sabhall* – a barn, just two miles north east

A pair of white oxen are said to have carried St Patrick to his grave, marked by this stone in the churchyard of Down Cathedral, Downpatrick

of Downpatrick, where St Patrick landed, has the ruins of the 12th-century Abbey founded by St Malachi on the site of a barn in which St Patrick celebrated his first mass in Ireland. At Struell, two miles east of Downpatrick, are St Patrick's Wells, originally Druidic waters, and blessed by the saint. Some hold that the blessed well waters will cure pilgrims suffering from eye ailments.

DOWNPATRICK is 22 miles from Belfast and 96 from Dublin.

THE GIANT'S CAUSEWAY
County Antrim

The rock formation of the Giant's Causeway ranks it as a geological structure of world interest. It is divided into the Honeycomb Causeway and the Little Causeway, a series of thousands of hexagonal vertical basalt columns assaulted by the sea. Bands of iron ore abound, and the causeway was formed by molten lava cooling as it burst through the earth's crust in the Cainozoic period. The various spectacular formations have been given fanciful names such as the Wishing Chair, My Lady's Fan, the Giant's Organ, the Giant's Loom and the Giant's Coffin. Fortunately Bushmills and its Distillery is only three miles south of the Causeway, which is not as 'Giant' as it is made out to be.

THE GIANT'S CAUSEWAY is the property of the National Trust and is 8 miles from Portrush, which is 60 miles from Belfast.

PORT-NA-BLAGH
County Donegal

Sheltered in Sheephaven Bay, this romantic and cosy little seaside resort has a splendid sandy beach and is an ideal centre from which to explore the exciting Atlantic Coast of the Rosguill Peninsular. Horn Head (600 ft of cliff), and Bloody Foreland, with Mount Errigal, the shining white and blue cone-shaped mountain (2466 ft) can be seen dominating the glorious landscape in the background like an Irish Fujiyama.

PORT-NA-BLAGH is just over 20 miles north west of Letterkenny and approximately 176 miles from Dublin, via Strabane.

ROSSNOWLAGH
County Donegal

Rossnowlagh has one of the finest and most beautiful strands and surfing beaches in the country. It has an excellent Museum of the County Donegal Historical Society, housed in the modern Franciscan Friary, which has lovely gardens and a beautiful church. The attractive Sand House Hotel is right on the water's edge, and the proprietress is Margaret Thatcher's double!

ROSSNOWLAGH is 133 miles from Dublin and 11 miles from Donegal town.

SHANE'S CASTLE
County Antrim

Shane's Castle has the unique distinction of having the only steam locomotive railway in regular service in Northern Ireland. The most popular amateur engine driver is the Lord Raymond O'Neill of Clannaboy. The railway runs all the way through his superb Nature Reserve, from Shane's Castle Station.

SHANE'S CASTLE is about 3 miles north of Antrim town, and about 17 miles from Belfast.

SLIGO
County Sligo

Sligo – Sligeac – The Shelley River, is a charming town on the south bank of the broad Garavogue River

Lord O'Neill with his gleaming steam train on the Shane's Castle Railway

Lough Gill, its waters smooth as glass, contains Yeats' magical Island of Innisfree

which links Lough Gill with the Atlantic ocean. Historically, it guarded the north-south main route on the west coast. It lies between the mountains of Benbulben and Knocknarea. The splendid ruins of Sligo Abbey date from 1641. The Sligo County Museum and Art Gallery has a special section of Yeats manuscripts, broadsheets and paintings, and is open to the public.

Lough Gill, just two miles from the town, contains the magical island of Innisfree which inspired Yeats' most famous poem *The Lake Isle of Innisfree*. On the south shore, near Cottage Island, is Dooney rock, made famous in Yeats' poem *The Fiddler of Dooney*. West of Sligo is Knocknarea (1078 ft), also featured in his poetry, on the summit of which is the huge burial cairn of Queen Maeve of Connacht. Five miles along the road from Sligo to Bundoran is Drumcliff. In its churchyard is the burial place of W.B. Yeats, with his own epitaph, 'Cast a cold Eye on Life, on Death. Horseman, pass by'. Two miles north of Drumcliff is Lissadell

House, open to the public, the home of the Gore-Booth family whose illustrious daughters were the poetess, Eva Gore-Booth, and Constance, Countess Markievicz, a leader of the 1916 Rising.

SLIGO is 135 miles from Dublin.

STRABANE
County Tyrone

Strabane, on the River Mourne, was the birthplace of John Dunlap, in 1747. He emigrated to Philadelphia in 1771 and founded the first daily newspaper in America, the *Pennsylvania Packet*. He printed the Declaration of Independence, served as a member of General Washington's bodyguard, and gave £4000 to his army. He served his time in Gray's printing press in Strabane, which is still in existence. James Wilson, grandfather of President Woodrow Wilson, also worked in Gray's printing works before emigrating to America in 1807.

STRABANE is 81 miles from Belfast, 18 miles from Letterkenny.

Flat-topped Benbulben in County Sligo

Index

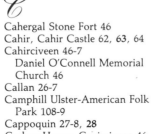

INDEX

Acknowledgements

Borde Fáilte: title page, contents 3, 4, 5, 6, 7(l,r), 8, 9(r), 11, 12, 13, 14, 15,
    16, 17, 18, 19, 20, 21, 22, 23, 25, 26, 27, 28, 29, 30, 31, 32, 33, 34(l,r), 35,
    36/7, 38, 39, 40, 41, 42, 43, 45, 46, 47, 48, 49, 50, 51(t,b), 52(t,b), 53,
    54/5, 56, 57, 58, 59, 61, 62, 63, 64, 65, 66, 67, 68, 69(l,r), 70, 71, 72/3,
    75, 76, 77, 78, 79, 80, 82/3, 84, 85, 86, 87(l,r) 89, 90/1, 93, 94, 95, 96,
    97, 98, 99, 100, 101, 102, 103, 108(b), 112, 113
John Freeman: 88
Northern Ireland Tourist Board: endpapers, title verso 105, 106, 107,
108(t), 109, 110, 111
Edward Pitcher: 9(l)